THE ECONOMICS OF EDUCATION

G.B.J.Atkinson

HODDER AND STOUGHTON
LONDON SYDNEY AUCKLAND TORONTO

British Library Cataloguing in Publication Data

Atkinson, G.B.J.
Economics of education.
1. Education—Economic aspects—Great Britain
I. Title
338.4′737′0941 LC67.G7

ISBN 0 340 33729 X

First published 1983

Printed in Great Britain for Hodder and Stoughton Educational, a division of Hodder and Stoughton Ltd, Mill Road, Dunton Green, Sevenoaks, Kent, by Clark Constable (1982) Ltd, Edinburgh.

Preface

This book has been in mind for a number of years. The movement from that nebulous state to something more durable was due to the help of a number of people, particularly my wife who also read and commented on the first draft. J. R. Hough, K. Drake and A. Hurst also read an early version and offered useful suggestions for improvement.

The librarians of Preston Polytechnic gave a service which was far beyond the requirements of duty.

Most of the typing was done by Sheila Wilkinson and by Rita Dickinson, Alison Ormsby and Laura Brown. I am grateful to them.

I should also like to thank the editors of the *Journal of Further and Higher Education* for allowing me to use material in Chapter 7 which first appeared there and the controller of Her Majesty's Stationery Office for permission to reproduce a chart in Chapter 5.

After all this help, the faults that appear are all my own.

To my mother, my wife Diana and to Rachel and Mark

Contents

Introduction

Educational policies are not determined by educational criteria alone. Whilst the views of teachers, inspectors and other educationalists are influential in some aspects of education such as the curricula, their views carry less weight in others. What happens in education is influenced by a wide variety of factors ranging from individual initiatives and historical precedents to the political and economic context within which the education system functions. This book is intended to illuminate some of the economic factors which affect education policy. It is intended primarily for those with some knowledge or interest in education who have no background in economics, and has been written so that where economic concepts or theories arise they are intelligable to the non-economist. I also hope that the book will be useful to those economists who are interested in education as an area for study.

The book is also an introduction to the economics of education. In other words it makes use of the techniques of economics and applies these to education. There are three main themes in this area of economics: the process by which education is 'produced', questions arising from the distribution of education in society, and problems associated with the finance of education.

Chapter 1 gives a brief historical survey of the growth of public spending on education in Britain, together with a more detailed look at recent spending. It also considers factors influencing variations in spending between local authorities. This leads to an analysis of costs in Chapter 2, making use of a number of concepts which may be unfamiliar to non-economists but which are important analytically. Chapter 3 considers the 'output' or benefits arising from education. These include not only knowledge but other consequences such as higher earnings; some of these are not necessarily beneficial, either to the individual or to society. Chapter 4 continues the themes of the previous chapters by introducing cost-benefit analysis and other aspects of the contribution which education can make to economic growth, such as the provision of skilled manpower. This is perhaps the most difficult chapter for the non-economist.

Chapter 5 is a kind of case study of one aspect of manpower planning. Teachers are the largest group of educated manpower in the country and shortages or over-production of teachers have obvious and important consequences for education.

Chapters 6 and 7 are linked. The first of these explains the theoretical and practical factors which influence the amount of money made available for spending on education. Chapter 7 looks at the views of some critics of the present system and considers briefly three alternatives – the provision of vouchers, student loans instead of grants, and the problem of equity in education.

The final chapter brings together many of the ideas discussed earlier in the book and looks at the thorny problem of efficiency in education through an examination of specific topics such as the use of educational technology and the size of classes and schools. The limits of an economic approach are apparent in this analysis.

Although the book does not specifically ask – or answer – the question 'What policies should be adopted in education?', it does seek to make clear the economic constraints and possibilities within which education operates and to show how economic analysis can influence education policy.

1
Expenditure on Education

Concept of Education

When the word 'education' is mentioned, the picture that springs to mind is of a school filled with children. In reality 'education' is a much wider concept than schooling, but it is difficult to define precisely. The Standard Industrial Classification divides the education industry into five groups – Higher Education, School Education, Education not elsewhere specified and vocational training, Driving and Flying schools and Research and Development.[1] Whilst this definition indicates the extent of the industry, it is not very helpful for the purpose of analysing public expenditure on education.

There are two main problem areas inherent in commenting on educational expenditure. The first of these is concerned with the agency that provides the education. This book is largely concerned with education provided by public bodies such as government and local authorities. However a considerable amount of education is provided by independent schools. It is difficult to be precise as to its importance, but in 1979 7.7% of the schools in England were independent and 5.6% of the pupils went to independent schools.[2] The amount spent on the education of these children is unknown, but clearly substantial. Another large area of spending which is difficult to measure is that provided by firms. Some in-service education of workers is provided or financed by organisations such as the Industrial Training Boards, but an unquantifiable amount of training is undertaken within firms, sometimes in the form of apprenticeships, but also in short courses or in less formal ways.

The difficulty in quantifying education provided by firms is a minor problem compared to quantifying education provided within the family. Much of the education provided within families does not involve expenditure of money, but of the time of parents helping their children in a variety of ways. Some expenditure is involved when families buy articles such as books, paper or pens for educational use. The distinction between 'education' and other family activities is a difficult one to make; is a trip to the zoo 'educational' or not? Many families do employ others to educate their children; for example when they pay piano teachers or for dance lessons. When all this activity is considered it is clear that expenditure on education is much larger than is commonly assumed.

So one problem area arises because education is provided by such a wide variety of bodies. However, even if we simplify the problem by limiting the analysis to publicly provided education, the distinctions are still not clear-cut. This is essentially a problem of definition. In making comparisons of expenditure we need to ensure that we are comparing like with like; but this is difficult to do. For example it would appear to be relatively straightforward to compare expenditure on primary education between authorities or with previous years. In practice even this cannot be done exactly because of the growth of middle schools which could be counted as either primary or secondary. Similarly in some authorities much post sixteen education is carried on in tertiary colleges and this makes it difficult to make fair comparisons of expenditure on secondary education.

Moreover the activities that count as education will vary with time and between countries. Welfare expenditure is an example of this; one could argue whether the school health service should be seen as educational spending. If it is, comparison between authorities becomes difficult, because in some areas there is a substantial provision whereas in others the same work would be undertaken by the Health Service. The problem of measurement is exacerbated because in this area of welfare provision there is considerable overlap between the activities of public authorities and of private charities. Even if the latter are excluded the problem of classification remains. Should expenditure on meals, or child guidance clinics be counted as educational? If school playing fields or gymnasiums are used by the general public should this count as expenditure on schools? Or again should expenditure on the library service be counted as educational?

Whatever decisions are made, it is clear that any classification is arbitrary. This makes it difficult to make comparisons with the past and with other countries where different classifications may be used, and it also creates problems of analysing current provision. Most of the following analysis is, therefore, concerned with a very narrow definition of education and attention is concentrated on provision by public authorities.

Historical Developments

The pioneering work in the UK on expenditure on education was undertaken by Vaizey and Sheehan and this section makes extensive use of their work.[3] They estimate that between 1920 and 1965 current expenditure on education in the UK rose from £65 million to £1115 million.[4] However this immense growth is misleading, for much of the increase was due to inflation. This difficulty can be overcome by re-calculating the actual expenditures into constant prices. In Table 1.1 all the expenditure has been changed to the prices prevailing in 1948 and so the table shows the growth in expenditure in real terms.

To make comparison even easier, these expenditures have been translated into index numbers, a technique often used by economists. The best known example of an index number is the Retail Price Index which is often used to measure inflation. It is difficult to compare the price of a basket of goods bought by a family and rising from £49.70 in one year to £54.17 the next and £57.15 in the following year. However, if we calculate that prices rose by £4.45 or 9% the first year, and that by the second year they had risen by 15%, we can produce index numbers. Spending in the base year is taken as 100 and the index shows the price of the basket of goods rising from 100 in the first year to 109 in the second and 115 in the third, making comparisons relatively easy.

In Table 1.1, expenditure in 1948 has been called 100 so the table shows that between 1948 and 1955 expenditure in real terms rose by 41%.

The main feature of this table is the huge increase in expenditure, which more than quadrupled in the forty five years. This increase was particularly rapid in the postwar period, especially after 1955. However, this growth was not constant, for expenditure in real terms fell between 1938 and 1945 as a result of war.

An alternative way of looking at educational expenditure during this

Table 1.1 *Expenditure in real terms on public education in the UK 1920 to 1965*

Year	*Expenditure £m. at 1948 prices*	*Index*
1920	100.2	47
1925	141.2	66
1930	152.9	71
1935	158.4	74
1938	165.0	77
1940	154.9	72
1945	144.6	67
1948	215.3	100
1950	263.0	122
1955	300.0	141
1965	451.4	210

Source: Vaizey, J., and Sheehan, J., *Resources for Education*, Allen & Unwin, 1968, p. 131.

period is to calculate expenditure on education as a share of national income. *National income* is a measure of the money value of the final goods and services produced by the economy during the year. It can be calculated in various ways, for example by adding together the total incomes received during the year, though *transfer incomes* such as pensions, which represent money transferred to some individuals from others without productive service, are excluded. An alternative way is to add up the output of all the industries and services in the economy. As the 'output' of education is difficult to measure, expenditure on education is used instead as a proxy for that output. The process enables us to calculate the changing share of education in the national income; that is, to look at the slice of the national cake going to education.

The figures in Table 1.2 must be treated with some caution. The problem of measuring education expenditure has already been discussed, but here the problem is compounded because estimates of national income are always inaccurate due to the difficulties of measuring such an enormous area of activity.

The table shows that the share of education rose quickly in the early 1920s, but then remained between 2% and 3% (with the exception of the war years) until the end of the 1950s when it rose substantially. The figures in Table 1.2 are for current expenditure only; the pattern is similar if capital expenditure is included, though the growth in the last period is even more pronounced. By 1965 the proportion of national income spent on education was exactly twice that of 1939.

Table 1.2 *Current net Public Expenditure as a proportion of the National Income in the UK 1920 to 1965*

Year ending	*Net National Income at Factor Cost £ million*	*Public Education Expenditure £ million*	*The share of Public Education %*
March			
1920	5512	65.1	1.2
1925	3934	84.1	2.1
1930	4122	92.8	2.3
1935	3938	92.7	2.4
1940	5272	107.5	2.0
1945	8359	143.9	1.7
1948	8593	215.3	2.5
1950	10239	272.0	2.7
1955	14668	410.6	2.8
1965	28279	1114.9	4.1

Source: Vaizey, J. and Sheehan, J., *op. cit.*, p. 139.

More Recent Developments

The changes in educational expenditure since the mid 1960s are summarised in Table 1.3. This can not be compared directly with the figures given earlier for various reasons. Firstly, Table 1.3 includes transfer expenditures such as student grants. Moreover this table is for England and Wales whilst earlier tables gave figures for the UK and were for calendar years. Column A shows a continuous growth in actual expenditure, but in part this reflects the effects of inflation. In column B, this influence is removed and actual expenditures have been converted to the price prevailing in 1980. The data shows that the growth discussed earlier for the 1950s and 1960s continued up to the mid 1970s. The trend then changed, and educational expenditure in real terms levelled out and even declined in some years. Another way to illustrate this is to use index numbers, and this is done in column C. The base year for this series of numbers is 1960 showing that expenditure on education more than doubled in real terms between 1960 and 1973/4.

The reasons for this changed pattern become clearer after consideration of Table 1.4 which looks at the UK as a whole. This confirms that public expenditure on education grew throughout the period, but this was partly caused by inflation. Until the mid 1970s two factors affected educational expenditure. The UK economy was growing richer as column D shows, and the *share* of education also grew. Then the position changed. The UK economy continued to grow (in most years) but at a much slower pace, and the share of education in national income actually fell. Apart from the war years this was the first fall in education's share this century.

Table 1.3 *Educational Expenditure in England & Wales*

Year	*A* *Actual Expenditure* *£ million*	*B* *Expenditure at* *1980 prices* *£ million*	*C* *Index of educational expenditure in real terms* *(1960 = 100)*
1968–69	1855	8526	158
1970–71	2273	9161	170
1972–73	3149	10378	192
1974–75	4697	11196	208
1976–77	6679	11503	213
1978–79	7752	11311	210
1980–81	10885	11172	207

Source: *Statistics of Finance and Awards*, DES, 1980, Table 1.

Table 1.4 *Education Expenditure and Gross National Product* (UK)

Year	*A* *Total Public Expenditure on Education (£ million)*	*B* *Gross National Product (£ million)*	*C* *A as % of B*	*D* *GNP Growth in real terms (1960 = 100)*
1968–69	2161	44607	5.0	127.0
1970–71	2648	52962	5.2	132.4
1972–73	3667	66802	5.6	140.8
1974–75	5472	89491	6.2	147.3
1976–77	7786	129803	6.0	150.8
1978–79	9054	170141	5.4	158.0
1980–81	12751	232284	5.5	155.8

Source: As Table 1.3

Explaining the Level of Spending

The actual amount of money spent on education is affected by many factors, but these can be subsumed under two: the demand of consumers – in this case parents and their children, and the amount which government is able and willing to supply.

One reason why more education was demanded was functional; in other words, the number of people to be educated increased. Although the number of children in primary schools was 4.3 million in both 1920 and 1965 there were considerable variations in the intervening years. More striking is that the number of children undergoing secondary education doubled from 1945 to 1955 and rose by a further million in the next decade.[5] This increase was in part a reflection of the birth rate, but it was also due to the raising of the school leaving age in 1947, as well as more children choosing to stay on at school. As secondary education is more expensive than primary this increase helped push up total expenditure by a substantial amount. Moreover, other very expensive areas of education grew rapidly. Thus the number of full-time students at British universities rose from 46000 to nearly 139000 in the period 1920 to 1965.[6] These functional causes of increased expenditure were reinforced because the rise in numbers was accompanied by an increasing complexity of things to be taught – in science for example – and in methods of teaching which laid stress on practical experimentation rather than chalk and talk. Both these developments were expensive.

However, the rise in expenditure was not solely due to functional reasons. Over the period as a whole national income rose and this meant that there were more resources available to be spent on education as well as on other activities. Education, however, was a substantial beneficiary of this growth for a number of reasons. There was a strong belief that the economy needed skilled manpower, and that expenditure on education was a wise investment for the country to make. This belief was reinforced by more personal considerations. People wanted 'the best' for their children and one way to achieve this was thought to be to give them a good start in life. So spending on education became politically popular as parents demanded ever better facilities for their children.

As their income rises, people spend proportionately more on some things and less on others. For example as families get richer they spend more on cars and less on public transport. They also spend proportionately more on foreign holidays, owner-occupied houses, meals in restaurants and on education. It is therefore not surprising that the years of rising national income were those in which educational expenditure rose even more quickly. A survey of spending in the richer countries of the world concluded 'the growth in educational expenditure is "explained" (in the statistical sense of the term) very completely by the trend of the economy for the whole of the period under consideration'.[7] As Table 1.5 shows, developed (i.e., rich) countries spent a greater proportion of their national income on education than did developing countries, though in both groups the share of education was increasing.

The increase in national income also affected the government's willingness to increase its spending on education. In a democratic society governments seek to respond to popular demand and, as more money was available, governments of all parties were willing to expand the education system – for example by creating new universities and expanding existing ones. They also spent more on 'improvements' to existing services by employing more teachers and so lowering the pupil-teacher ratio.

During the 1970s a number of factors changed. The birth rate had been falling since 1964, so that during the 1970s and 1980s many schools found they had fewer children to be educated. National income grew more slowly and even fell. This affected individual and public willingness and ability to spend money on education and it also caused

Table 1.5 *International Public Expenditure on Education*

	Total Spending $ million		*As % of GNP*		*Per inhabitant $*	
	1965	*1979*	*1965*	*1979*	*1965*	*1979*
Developed Countries	87239	464187	5.1	5.9	85	403
Developing Countries	7746	65595	2.9	4.0	5	31
World Total	94985	529782	4.8	5.6	38	162

Source: UNESCO, *Statistical Yearbook*, 1982, Table 2.12.

governments to re-appraise their spending on education. In part this was because the government had to spend more on other things such as unemployment benefit, but it also reflected a change in government attitudes, particularly after the Conservative victory in the 1979 General Election. There was a growing scepticism about the value of public spending and a belief that governments ought to intervene less in the life of the country. This ideology led to strenuous efforts to cut government spending and education was affected by these cuts.

Local Government Expenditure on Education

Most of the spending on education in England and Wales is undertaken by local authorities and there are considerable variations between authorities. For example, in 1982/83 estimates of expenditure per pupil in primary schools varied from £556 to £1025 with a mean of £649. For secondary schools the average per pupil expenditure was £903, but the lowest was £748 and the highest £1427, the highest often occurring in London.[8] One cause of these differences is that teachers in the London area receive a special salary allowance and this puts up the cost of education. However this factor alone is not enough to explain the differences, and there have been a number of attempts to explain the variations, largely by looking for correlations between expenditure on education and other factors. Correlation analysis is a statistical technique which measures the relationship between two variables. For example, as temperature rises so does spending on ice cream, and this relationship can be measured. However, the fact that two variables show a high correlation does not necessarily mean that a change in one would cause the other to vary. There would probably be a high correlation between the number of people flying the Atlantic over the last twenty years and the sales of consumer durable goods such as colour televisions. Clearly there is no cause and effect here. Both have increased due to rises in the standard of living which means that more people can afford to fly and to buy televisions. In the case of some high correlations, however, it is not clear whether the statistical relationship is due to chance, or to some outside cause, or whether it represents cause and effect. Thus correlational evidence must be treated with some caution.

An early study in this area was by Davies who examined the expenditure of county boroughs in 1961/62 and found, as expected, that the level of spending was associated with the number of children. High spending per pupil was associated with social factors, such as the number of immigrants and the proportion of families with shared dwellings. Spending per pupil was lower the higher the proportion of school children in the area, or to put it another way, areas with a high proportion of adults and relatively few children tended to spend more on each child.[9] More recently, Boaden found that in county boroughs Labour councils spend more than Conservatives when other factors were allowed for.[10] This result was supported by Alt's research when he examined spending in county boroughs over a decade. Labour Party control was associated with more spending in both primary and secondary schools. Another factor affecting spending was the rateable value per head in an area so that 'rich' areas spent more.[11]

Since local government reorganisation, there have been a number of studies. Dawson found that those authorities with many schools spent more than average. Other significant factors were the proportion of immigrants and people living in houses lacking in basic amenities.[12] The work of Foster *et al.* suggests that the number of owner occupiers as a proportion of total households is inversely related to expenditure on education in both primary and secondary education; that is, if other factors are held constant, areas with many owner occupiers tend to spend less on education. More is spent where household incomes are high.[13] Similar results were obtained by Howick and Hassani who analysed local authority spending in the late 1970s. Their research confirms the wide variation in expenditure mentioned earlier. Expenditure in primary education was positively correlated with variables such as the number of immigrants, one parent families, and with overcrowding, suggesting that spending tends to be higher in areas suffering from adverse conditions. Labour controlled councils tended to spend more than Conservative, but not when the figures were adjusted to hold the socio-economic variables constant. In a later analysis of expenditure on secondary education they found similar results but the correlations were much weaker, especially outside London.[14]

Another analysis of school spending was undertaken by Hough. He investigated the possible effect of different types of local authority (e.g. county council, metropolitan district) on spending on education. As might be expected total expenditure per pupil was correlated negatively with the pupil/teacher ratio, but positively with the average teacher's salary. Areas with a high adult to child ratio spent more on education in the county councils, but less in those metropolitan district councils without middle schools. Comparing all county councils with all metropolitan districts, the county councils have higher levels of expenditure per pupil partly because their teachers receive higher salaries on average. On the other hand the county councils have less favourable pupil/teacher ratios and spend less per head of population – that is, less is spent for each inhabitant in the area.[15]

Despite all this research it is not possible to state clearly the determinants of educational expenditure between authorities. Some factors are obvious: an authority with a generous pupil/teacher ratio will probably spend more on education than one where the ratio is smaller. There is clearly some freedom of manoeuvre for individual authorities to determine how much they spend: thus Labour controlled authorities tend to spend more. It is not clear though why social factors such as the number of immigrants or the proportion of families with shared dwellings should significantly affect spending on education. The research therefore amounts to little more than a list of items which seem to be associated with more or less spending, leaving no adequate theory to explain the pattern or enable predictions of future spending to be made.

So far this discussion has been concerned with gross figures; but educated people retire or die or leave the labour force in other ways and some education is 'lost' as knowledge becomes obsolescent. One attempt to estimate this net investment was undertaken by Scott who analysed UK data from 1951 to 1971.[16] His results suggest that in this period the volume of net investment increased between three and five times, depending on the methodology used.

It is clear that in the long run spending on education in Britain, as in the rest of the world, has increased enormously. Over the century as a whole, education has been one of the growth industries, though in recent years this growth has slowed down or even reversed.

There are considerable spatial variations in educational expenditure, and a number of researchers have discovered correlations between spending and other characteristics such as wealth, or political control, but there is no real explanation of most of these findings. The correlations may sometimes be due to chance, and spending may vary according to individual initiatives in particular authorities.

References

1 *Standard Industrial Classification*, Central Statistical Office, HMSO, 1980, p. 66–67.
2 DES, *Statistical Bulletin*, 17/81, November 1981.
3 Vaizey, J. and Sheehan, J., *Resources for Education*, Allen & Unwin, 1968.
4 *ibid*, p. 139.
5 *ibid*, p. 4.
6 *ibid*, p. 126.
7 *Trends in Educational Expenditure in the OECD Countries*, OECD, 1978, p. 20.
8 *Education Estimates* 1982/1983, CIPFA, July 1983, pp. 82–83.
9 Davies, B. P., *Social Needs and Resources in Social Services*, Michael Joseph, 1968, Ch. 12.
10 Boaden, N., *Urban Policy Making: Influences on County Boroughs in England and Wales*, Cambridge University Press, 1971, Ch. 5.
11 Alt, J. E., 'Some Social and Political Correlates of County Borough Expenditure' *B.J. Political Science*, Vol. 1, Pt 1, 1971.
12 Dawson, D. A., 'Determinants of Local Government Expenditure',

Appendix 7 of the *Report of the Committee of Enquiry into Local Government Finance* (the Layfield Report), HMSO, 1977.

13 Foster, C. D., Jackman, R. and Perlman, M., *Local Government Finance in a Unitary State*, Allen & Unwin, 1980, p. 269.

14 Howick, C. and Hassani, H. 'Education Spending: Primary' *Centre for Environmental Studies Review*, Vol. 5, 1979, pp. 41–48, and 'Secondary', Vol. 8, 1980, pp. 25–30.

15 Hough, J. R., *A Study of School Costs*, NFER-Nelson, 1981, Ch. 5.

16 Scott, M., 'Investment in Education in the UK 1951–1971' *Oxford Review of Education*, Vol. 6, No. 1, 1980, pp. 21–30.

2

Costs

Direct Costs

Economists have a number of ways of examining costs. One of these is to differentiate between direct and indirect costs. The word 'direct' is used to indicate that these are spent directly by students or by public authorities on such items as teachers' salaries or books. These costs are directly attributable to education whereas 'indirect' costs tend to be implicit. For example a student's time is valuable and is part of the cost of education, though it is not paid for directly. These indirect costs may have to be allocated in a rather arbitrary manner because they are shared with other activities. Thus part of central government general administration costs are allocated to education indirectly. These indirect costs are examined later.

Direct costs receive most attention because the figures are fairly easily available, and because such spending affects the level of taxation. When these issues are discussed, attention is usually concentrated on *total costs*. This is the figure that is of most concern to such bodies as local authorities who have to pay the bills. The prime determinant of total cost is the rate of output. Just as it costs more to produce a thousand chairs than five hundred, so the total cost of educating a thousand children will be more than that of educating five hundred. This does not mean that costs will necessarily rise proportionately; a school for a thousand children may be twice as expensive as one for five hundred but it may be more or less than that.

Table 2.1 shows the total costs of education in England and Wales. Whilst the details vary, the pattern of expenditure is similar in most other countries. Thus the largest two items are secondary and primary schools, which amount to approximately 55% of total expenditure. This figure will vary with the circumstances. Thus, if the number of children of school age falls, the proportion of total expenditure spent on schools will also tend to fall; if more children stay on after the compulsory school

Table 2.1 *Public Authorities' Expenditure on Education by Type of Service in England and Wales 1980/81.*

	£ millions	*% of Total*
Nursery Schools	41	0.4
Primary Schools	2751	23.8
Secondary Schools	3693	31.9
Special Schools	452	3.9
Further and Adult	1661	14.3
Training of Teachers – tuition	46	0.4
Universities	1157	10.0
Other	448	3.9
Related Expenditure	1319	11.4
Total	11568	100.0

Source: *Statistics of Finance and Awards*, DES, 1980, Table 2.

Notes: 1 The table excludes expenditure on libraries and museums; expenditure by the Department of Education and Science on teachers' superannuation, and expenditure on education by other government departments (e.g. by the armed forces).

2 'Related Expenditure' includes such items as school health (£21 m), meals and milk (£440 m), the youth service (£129 m), maintenance grants to pupils and students (£524 m) and transport of pupils/students (£180 m).

3 These figures include loan charges.

leaving age, it will rise. This will also affect the proportion of money spent on various sectors. The share of total expenditure undertaken by schools has fallen over the last half century though the share of secondary education has tended to grow for a variety of reasons, such as the raising of the school leaving age and because more pupils have chosen to stay on at school.[1] There has thus been a substantial switch of educational expenditure towards the older age groups who are often those with educational or social advantages, since those likely to stay on at school or go to college are rather more likely to be cleverer or to come from middle class homes.

The figures however must be treated with some caution. Firstly, the figures in Table 2.1 are high, partly because they include capital expenditure and loan charges which would be excluded from some statistics. Moreover, the allocation of expenditure is sometimes arbitrary. For example adult education often makes use of schools but it is not clear how accommodation costs should be allocated. Practice also varies between authorities. In some areas, items such as architects' fees for new buildings would be counted as current expenditure, in others as a capital charge.

Whilst total costs are of great significance to those paying bills they are not necessarily particularly useful for more analytical purposes, for example in attempting to make comparisons. Here *average cost* per pupil is more helpful, and in much economic analysis of education the most common approach is to calculate what it costs to educate one pupil or student for a year.

Primary education can be seen to be a relatively inexpensive sector of education. The figure for nursery education is particularly interesting. It is very high due to the 'generous' number of adults per child and this may be the prime reason why provision of nursery schools is so poor. At times when finance is – or seems to be – scarce it requires very strong reasons to expand such an expensive sector of education.

The changes in average cost during the decade can only be fully understood by making use of another concept: that of *marginal cost.* The marginal cost of any activity is the cost of producing an extra unit of output. Thus if a furniture firm produces ten tables at a total cost of £500 and then increases production so that it makes eleven tables at a total cost of £530 the marginal cost of the eleventh table is £30. An educational example would be the cost of an additional child in an existing classroom. Thus if a class has twenty children and one additional child is added the marginal cost will be the extra cost of educating this twenty first child. This may be much less than the average cost, for the extra child will not require any extra money spent on teachers, caretakers, cleaners, secretaries, light or heat.

Although the concept of marginal cost is not difficult, difficulties do arise in attempting to calculate it for particular institutions. As Hough points out, the term 'margin' has a certain flexibility and could encompass such variations as one extra pupil in the school, or the addition of an optional subject to the timetable, or an extra tutor group. In each case the marginal cost would depend on the amount of spare capacity in the school and this makes comparisons and calculations difficult.[2] However attempts have been made. Selby Smith analysed costs in British colleges of further education and made use of differing definitions of marginal cost. Firstly, it was defined as the addition to total financial cost due to educating one additional student in an existing under-used course. His second definition was the addition to total financial cost of educating an additional student if courses had to be duplicated, and this was accompanied by some improvements in efficiency. Selby Smith found very wide variations of marginal cost between courses and between definitions but in every case marginal costs using definition one were much lower than average costs.[3] If children could be allocated to schools or students to courses where vacant places exist in existing classes, opportunities for substantial savings would occur. There are, of course, difficulties in attempting this, and disadvantages may arise for the children concerned.

Table 2.2 provides an example of the use of marginal cost. It shows that there has been a substantial fall in the average cost of educating a polytechnic student. One reason for this is that classes have grown in size

Table 2.2 *Net Recurrent Institutional Expenditure in England and Wales in 1975/76 and 1980/81 £ per student*

	1975/76	*1980/81*	*% change*
Nursery Schools[1]	n.a.	1090	—
Primary Schools	539	608	13
Secondary Schools:			
pupils under compulsory school leaving age	783	813	4
pupils over compulsory school leaving age	1433	1364	–5
Further Education (non advanced work)	1709	1855	6
Polytechnics (advanced work)[1]	4136	3397	–18
Universities	4029	4293	7

Source: *Statistics of Finance and Awards,* DES, 1980, Table 2.

Notes: 1 Data for the earlier period is not available for nursery schools.
2 The figures for universities are for Great Britain, not just England and Wales.
3 The fall in costs for 16+ pupils was partly due to changes in the age structure of this group.
4 These prices are in November 1981 pounds, so that the effects of inflation are removed.

and the additional students admitted have added relatively little to total costs. Exactly the opposite has happened in primary schools. There, numbers of pupils fell during the decade. In some cases this meant that classes or schools could be closed, but it usually just meant that the number of children in the class fell. As each class still needed teachers and other items such as light and heat, the reduction in numbers had little effect on total cost, but pushed up average costs substantially. Thus, using the figures in Table 2.2, a primary class of thirty children in 1975–76 would cost £539 × 30 = £16 170 per annum. If total costs stayed the same but numbers fell to twenty-seven, the average cost would be approximately £600, that is roughly the figure for 1980–81. This example is, of course, oversimplified, for there were other changes during the decade which influenced average costs, such as changes in teachers' salaries. Moreover, one reason for the increase in spending on the average secondary school pupil was that schools introduced more expensive equipment such as video recorders, computers and photocopiers.

As with earlier tables, the figures must be treated with some caution. For example, the table suggests that the cost of educating a student at a polytechnic was substantially less than at a university. This does not necessarily mean that polytechnics are more efficient; the difference may arise because universities mount different and more expensive courses such as medical training, or because proportionally more staff time is spent on non-student activities such as research.

Another way to analyse the costs of education is by function. This is done in Table 2.3. The most significant feature of this table is the dominating nature of salaries, particularly those of teachers. Education is a very labour intensive industry. This fact becomes particularly significant at times when governments seek to cut public expenditure. If education is one of the areas asked to reduce spending, the burden must fall heavily on salaries because they form such a substantial part of the whole and because 'other costs' includes a wide variety of essential items which are relatively small. The table may be slightly misleading in this context however, because it is concerned with *institutional* costs and therefore ignores items such as County Hall expenditure.

As can be seen from the table, the proportion spent on teachers' salaries falls under 50% only in the cases of the two extremes. For nursery schools this is because a large part of the spending goes on adults other than teachers, such as nursery nurses. In the case of universities skilled workers, such as technicians, take up a higher proportion of spending than in other institutions, and the equipment, under 'other costs', is sophisticated and expensive.

It must be remembered that these figures are average and there will be very wide variations from these figures for individual institutions. Thus Hough concluded:

> within any one group of broadly comparable schools within any one LEA in any one year, average cost per pupil usually differs greatly from one school to another; in a number of cases twice or three times as much per pupil is spent at one school as at another . . . Teachers' salaries clearly dominate total costs although their percentage con-

Table 2.3 *Gross Recurrent Institutional Expenditure per Student, 1980–81*

	Teachers' Salaries		*Other Wages*		*Other Costs*		*Total*
	£	%	£	%	£	%	£
Nursery Schools	443	45	391	39	157	16	991
Primary	385	70	66	12	98	18	549
Secondary (USLA)	514	70	75	10	148	20	737
Secondary (OSLA)	874	71	122	10	240	19	1236
Special	1405	57	630	25	439	18	2474
Further Education (non advanced)	1068	64	272	16	339	20	1679
Polytechnics (advanced)	1621	53	708	23	754	24	3083
Universities	1685	40	1167	27	1392	33	4244

Source: *Statistics of Finance and Awards*, DES, 1980, Table 11.

Note: These figures are *gross*. They are higher than the figures in Table 2.2 because those gave the net recurrent cost to public funds. The difference is income received which was relatively large for sectors such as universities.

Another difference is that these figures are for actual expenditures in 1980–81 whilst those in Table 2.2 were increased to November 1981 prices.

tribution to the latter was found to vary from 48 per cent to 66 per cent for different sub-groups of schools.[4]

This conclusion is supported by data from other sources. Cumming analysed Scottish school costs and found that the outlay per pupil in some areas was twice as high as in other areas. The main cause of this difference was geographical, for the 'heath and moor' counties, such as Sutherland or Ross and Cromarty, were much more expensive than the city or industrial areas. Cumming found that the proportion spent on teachers' salaries varied between 42% and 48%. The difference between these figures and those of Hough was due in part to different definitions of total cost.[5]

One difficulty that usually arises in comparing school costs is that the schools themselves vary. In Cumming's case there were substantial geographical differences; in others there are differences in kind of school (comprehensive, selective) or in the age of children. Thus 'secondary' schools can include pupils aged 11–18, or 11–16 or 13–18. Moreover, there may be differences between authorities if some are more generous than others. However, even when all these factors are held constant there are still considerable variations between schools as Table 2.4 indicates.

The data in this table was obtained from a large local education authority in the North of England. In order to reduce the influence of extraneous factors, such as those discussed above, the analysis was limited to those schools for pupils aged 11–16 years which had been comprehensive for five years or more. This gave a sample of forty-four schools with a total of over 8500 pupils. The schools included some from urban and some from rural areas and varied in size from 502 pupils to 1093. The figures refer to school based costs, and therefore omit other expenditure such as administration and inspection which arise outside the schools. Expenditure on school meals has also been excluded.

Clearly, even when many factors are held constant, there are large differences on expenditure. The most important item was teachers' salaries which amounted to 75% of total costs, and variations in this may arise because some schools are 'overstaffed', or because the staff are

Table 2.4 *Expenditure per Pupil in 11–16 Comprehensive Schools in One Authority* *£ per pupil 1978/79*

	Teachers' Salaries	*Other Wages*	*Premises*	*Equipment*	*Books*	*Printing & Stationary*	*Total*
Most Expensive	416	82	136	7	7	19	665
Mean	358	45	53	3	4	11	474
Least Expensive	307	32	24	0	3	7	373
% of total	75	10	11	1	1	2	100

more experienced and therefore at the top end of the salary scales. 'Overstaffing' can arise for example because pupil numbers are declining while staff do not leave. Whilst expenditure on teachers explained most of the variation in total cost, proportionately other expenditure varies more. This can arise because schools have different designs and may need to spend more or less on light and heat; or they may have large expenditure on items such as furniture in any one year. In recent years expenditure on books has received considerable attention and the figures here show large variation between schools. This variation is not exceptional; a DES survey of maintained secondary schools in England in 1978/79 showed large variations in expenditure on books. Over a quarter of middle-sized schools spent less than £50 per 100 pupils whilst ten per cent spent over £250 per 100 pupils. Part of this variation is explained because schools containing older pupils tend to spend more than 11–16 secondary schools.[6]

Indirect Costs

So far we have been discussing direct costs where money is handed over directly to pay for some activity. This is the everyday notion of what is meant by cost, but it is only a partial view. Economists are concerned with the allocation of resources, and viewed in this perspective the real cost of anything is that which is given up to obtain it. This is called the *opportunity cost.* Thus if a child has to choose between an ice cream and an ice lolly and chooses the latter, its real cost – what is given up – is the ice cream. Similarly the opportunity cost of reading this book is the value of the activity which would have been undertaken in its place. Most direct costs are also opportunity costs, because the money paid to buy such items as books is usually a fairly good measure of what could be obtained instead of the books. However the opportunity cost of something also includes the implicit or indirect costs, that is, the estimated cost of other scarce resources which are used but which are not entered into the account or paid for directly. The classic example of such an indirect cost is the value of student's time. Pupils or students beyond the minimum school leaving age who are in full-time education could have been at work, and so the opportunity cost of their time is the earnings foregone.

Opportunity cost is a relatively simple concept, but one which has powerful implications. As Drake points out, educational decision making becomes a matter of choosing between the alternative uses to which *all* scarce resources can be put, and not merely those resources which, through the accident of social structure, happen to be priced.[7] The cost of one method of teaching includes the foregone benefits which would have occurred if an alternative method of teaching had been used. In this case the opportunity cost is the learning foregone. Similarly time spent by teachers on routine clerical activities such as typing or duplicating has a high opportunity cost which ought to be considered when planning the efficient allocation of resources. Whilst the practical difficulties of providing adequate clerical assistance in schools at the time and place where they are needed may be substantial, there is a strong economic case in principle for the attempt to be made. Classroom materials typed and duplicated by teachers are very expensive materials.

The principle of opportunity costing has other implications for the efficient operation of educational institutions. At present we run schools and colleges as if student time was a free and costless resource such as air. A class waiting for a teacher is in fact using up a valuable resource – time. Similarly, the reluctance of staff to attend meetings after school hours, or of many adults to take up places on highly subsidised courses, indicates the substantial value people place on their leisure time. Opportunity cost also helps to explain why many children leave school as soon as legally possible.

Whilst the principle of opportunity cost is generally recognised, the attempt to quantify actual cases is a matter of some controversy. The principal opposition has come from Vaizey. He argues that students do not think in terms of income foregone, and points out the considerable difficulties involved in actually measuring income foregone.[8] Young people are legally prohibited from working below some specified age in almost every country. Thus the situation arises that their time is valuable – certainly to them – but they cannot work (except part-time) and their earnings foregone are therefore zero. Moreover if all, or even a substantial number of students, were to leave education and seek work, the unemployment rate for this group would rise and some students would have zero (or very low) foregone earnings. Becker counters this first argument by suggesting that if foregone earnings are to be excluded because education is compulsory then direct costs should equally be excluded.[9] Vaizey's point concerning an increase in unemployment is largely concerned with the problem of measurement rather than the decision to include these costs, though Bowman claims that no adjustment should be made for unemployment because the intention is to measure resource use rather than the failure to use them.[10]

The weight of the argument seems clear. Opportunity costs are real costs, student time is a real resource and should be included in any analysis of the costs of education. However, it is easier to state the principle than to realise it, for there are very substantial difficulties involved in any attempt actually to measure these costs. The first difficulty is lack of data. People in the United Kingdom are in general reluctant to divulge their earnings, and as a result governments are wary of using enquiries such as the census to obtain this data. Thus a good deal of information is available about earnings in particular occupations or industries, but very little of this is related to education and that is what is needed in this instance. In an attempt to measure the earnings foregone of university graduates we would need details of the earnings of people of similar age with similar qualifications who had not gone to university. The data would be needed separately for men and women, since despite legislation, pay is not equal in practice. For such a large and important group as this, data of some kind is available. The problem is much worse when smaller groups are considered; what, for example, would be the earnings foregone of women students taking PhDs in engineering?

Even where data exists, difficulties arise. The majority of young people who go into full-time education may have more ability than others not in full-time education. Using earnings for the latter could underestimate earnings foregone, since if the students had actually gone out to work then their ability could have given them higher earnings. To some extent this problem is mitigated because the actual earnings of those at work will be under reported as they too may undergo some training, the costs of which are born by the firm.[11]

Another problem concerns unemployment. Particularly when this is widespread, many people attending courses would otherwise be unemployed and it is therefore misleading to calculate their earnings foregone as what they would earn if working. One writer claims that the estimation of earnings foregone is the weakest component of economic analysis of manpower programmes because of the underestimation of unemployment. This is perhaps true in some situations, such as short term training programmes where a high proportion of participants are unemployed.[12]

The problem of estimating opportunity costs is particularly acute when leisure time is concerned. For some courses time given up to study is almost entirely leisure time; this would be the case for Open University students and for those attending evening classes. For some students time given up is part work time and part leisure, for example where classes are held in work time but homework has to be done in the evening. The position is further complicated because there is evidence to suggest that young people in school work substantially fewer hours than do otherwise comparable young people out of school.[13]

Even if the amount of leisure time given up could be ascertained with some accuracy, the problem of what value to give it would remain. Since some people can choose to work longer or shorter hours, it can be argued that for these people an hour of leisure time could be measured roughly by the overtime rate; that is the income they receive for giving up leisure. For particular groups such as teachers, a pragmatic approach may be to use the amount they would earn teaching evening classes. In general the best approach may be to adopt O'Donoghue's suggestion that despite its limitations the wage rate is the best approximation.[14]

So far this chapter has been concerned with the analysis of the costs of education from the point of view of society as a whole. In some cases it is also appropriate to analyse costs from the perspective of the individual concerned. This is particularly important when analysing such problems as what factors influence children to stay on at school. Private costs differ substantially from those of society, because for most courses the direct costs are subsidised from public funds and the effect of earnings foregone may be mitigated by students' grants. Moreover the individual will be concerned with income after tax. Thus the private costs of education are usually much lower than the social. The individual may well have to lose earnings, and have to pay extra travel and other costs, but these are relatively small.

A frequent comment made during this analysis of costs has been that there are difficulties in measurement; this is perhaps the prime difficulty in an economic approach to education. Techniques such as cost benefit analysis depend on the use of actual figures and inaccurate or unobtainable figures leave these efforts open to a good deal of scepticism.

Capital Costs

The distinction between current costs discussed earlier, and capital costs is not precise. It could be argued that goods such as books which last several years could be counted as capital equipment, but these are almost always counted as current expenditure, though more expensive items such as vehicles or computers are treated differently. In practice the distinction between current and capital goods is often one of administrative convenience where expensive and long-lasting items are paid for out of a separate budget. One item that is always treated differently is new buildings and this is the best example of a capital item.

From an economic point of view, building costs provide an example of both direct and indirect costs. The direct costs arise because builders and others are paid directly for their services, though analytical difficulties arise because the building will be in use over a number of years. For planning purposes this may be assumed to be sixty years.[15] Thus the annual depreciation cost of a building costing six million pounds would be £6 million divided by 60 = £100 000. If the building was occupied by 1000 students the annual cost per student would be £100. However, there is also an opportunity cost; if the money had not been used for this purpose it could have been allocated to other purposes, or the money could have been invested and interest received. This interest may be used as a measure of the opportunity cost. Thus if interest rates are 10% on a building of £6 million, the earnings foregone on the building are £600 000 or £600 per student for 1000 students. Thus the total capital cost per student would be £700 per annum.

There have been few studies of capital costs, for the good reason that it appears that no local education authority keeps records of the outstanding capital charges for each school, for authorities usually borrow in bulk and they could not apportion a particular loan to a particular school. In any case, historic costs may not be particularly useful if costs are being analysed as part of a cost-benefit analysis, which is concerned with planning future investment. However, to some extent there are economies of size, because for much of the post war period the Department of Education and Science stipulated fixed cost ceilings for school buildings which allowed less per place for large buildings.[16] One study of capital costs of secondary schools was undertaken by Norris, though his sample was a mere six schools of varying sizes. That work suggests that capital costs are around 18% of the total costs of secondary schools.[17] This figure must be treated with a good deal of scepticism because of the small sample.

Capital cost analysis can have practical results. Shortly after the Second World War a comparative study of recent school building costs in the UK was undertaken. This showed wide variations in cost per square foot. As a result of further studies ways were devised to rationalise school construction costs and in 1950 cost limits established on all new schools. The regulations set appropriate standards and left room for choice by local authorities but reduced costs, for example by encouraging the design and production of standardised components for school buildings. Over twenty years a rough estimate suggests that around six hundred million pounds was saved through the use of these techniques.[18]

Putting together all these costs, it is possible to draw up a cost per student from the standpoint of society. This is done in Table 2.5. The costs are hypothetical, but are roughly those appertaining to a full-time student in a polytechnic or university on an undergraduate course. Student grants are not included because these are a 'transfer' rather than a real cost. In other words the real cost to society of a student is what he would have produced if he had been working. This is measured by his wage. The student grant is just a transfer from one group (taxpayers) to another (students).

Table 2.5 *Hypothetical Social Costs of a Full-time Student*

	£ per annum
Direct cost	3000
Earnings foregone	3500
Capital	700
Total	7200

Note that no adjustment has been made here for unemployment or for ability.

Table 2.6 *Hypothetical Private Costs of a Full-time Student*

	£ per annum
Tuition[1]	100
Extra Meals and Travel[2]	200
Net Earnings Foregone[3]	3000
Total	3300

Notes: 1 The 'tuition' item consists of extra books and stationery that would not otherwise have been bought.
2 This assumes that some extra meals and journeys are necessary.
3 Net earnings foregone is made up of the (say) £3500 he would have earned, less tax.
4 These costs are mitigated by various receipts such as student grant and vacation earnings.

Whilst the figures in Table 2.5 are hypothetical, they do indicate the great importance of earnings foregone.

So far as the individual student is concerned, the figures would seem very different. Table 2.6 illustrates the same situation from a private point of view.

The figures in Tables 2.5 and 2.6 are rough estimates of costs around 1980. They will show considerable variation from student to student. Despite the approximation it is clear that private costs of education are substantially less than those to society.

When discussing student costs in this chapter it has been implicitly assumed that the output of each sector of education is homogeneous, for example, that all university students represent an identical output. This is as untrue as would be the assumption of a builder that houses cost £30 000 to build. In practice the cost will vary with the type and situation of the house. Clearly it is not possible to progress very far in analysing costs without looking at what is being produced; in other words at output.

References

1 Vaizey, J. and Sheehan, J., *Resources for Education*, Allen & Unwin, 1968, p. 136.
2 Hough, J. R., *A Study of School Costs*, NFER, 1981, pp. 133–34.

3 Smith, C. Selby, *The Costs of Further Education*, Pergamon, 1970, pp. 57–59.
4 Hough, J. R., *op. cit.*, pp. 139–40.
5 Cumming, C. E., *Studies in Educational Cost*, Scottish Academic Press, 1971, Table 2.5.
6 DES, 'Secondary School Library Service' *Statistical Bulletin* 7/81, May 1981.
7 Drake, K., 'The Importance of Costing Adult Education', *Studies in Adult Education*, Vol. 4, No. 2, October 1972, p. 128.
8 Vaizey, J., *The Political Economy of Education*, Duckworth, 1972, p. 224.
9 Becker, G. S., *Human Capital: A Theoretical and Empirical Analysis*, Princeton University Press, 1964, p. 74.
10 Bowman, M. J., 'The Costing of Human Resource Development', *Economics of Education*, eds Robinson, E. A. E., and Vaizey, J., Macmillan, 1966.
11 Mincer, J., 'On the job training: Costs Returns and Some Implications', *Journal of Political Economy*, Vol. LXX, October 1962, pp. 50–79.
12 Smith, R. E., 'The Opportunity Cost of Participating in a Training Programme', *Journal of Human Resources*, Vol. vi, No. 4, Fall 1971, pp. 510–19.
13 Parsons, D. O., 'The Cost of School Time, Foregone Earnings and Human Capital Formation', *Journal of Political Economy*, Vol. 82, No. 2, Pt 1, March/April 1974, pp. 251–66.
14 O'Donoghue, M., *Economic Dimensions in Education*, Gill & Macmillan, 1971, p. 53.
15 The method described here is that in *Student Numbers in Higher Education in England and Wales*, Education Planning Paper No. 2, HMSO, 1970.
16 Hough, J. R., *op. cit.*, p. 152.
17 Vaizey, J., Hewton, E. and Norris, K., *The Costs of New Educational Technologies,* Gulbenkian Institute, Lisbon, 1971, p. 17f.
18 Coombs, P. H. and Hallak, J., *Managing Educational Costs*, Oxford University Press, 1972, pp. 57–61.

3

The Output of Education

The Kinds of Output

Oscar Wilde defined a cynic as a man who knows the price of everything and the value of nothing and this may seem an apt comment on those economists who seek to measure the output of education. Many educators find the notion of output rather alien as it seems to relegate education to the position of a candy floss factory. Clearly many of the outcomes of education are difficult to measure, let alone to price, but an analysis of the results or benefits of education can be to its advantage.

One approach to the analysis of the output of education is typified by Wagner in his examination of higher education.[1] The first output he identifies is 'the furtherance of civilisation'. This involves encouraging the rediscovery of man's highest creative achievements, making new discoveries and questioning old ones. Clearly this objective cannot be measured, though academics might attempt to evaluate an institution using standard academic criteria.

A related activity is that of research. Although this is usually visualised as the discovery of new knowledge, it also includes the restructuring and application of existing knowledge. There are various approaches to measuring the research output of an institution, such as counting the number of books and articles published by its staff, but in practice it is impossible to achieve a satisfactory measure of the value of research.

The most obvious function of universities and other educational institutions is to provide teaching, and this gives rise to several outputs. One is to select people for subsequent employment; higher education acts as a filter or screen. Alternatively, teaching can be seen as an aid to maturation; to provide resources so that individuals will mature and develop, and teaching plays some part in this. However, the main output of teaching for most people would be seen as knowledge, broadly defined to include such things as skills and values. This could in principle be measured by giving tests to students at the beginning and end of the course to measure the knowledge added. Apart from the administrative difficulties of such a procedure, there are insurmountable problems in developing satisfactory tests for all courses, though adequate ones could perhaps be developed for some. So whilst this procedure does offer possibilities it too has considerable limitations. An alternative approach is to use the value subsequent employers place on the knowledge gained by students. This is discussed in the next section.

This brief analysis clearly suggests that it is not possible to measure the outputs of education in a satisfactory way using this kind of approach. Even if it were possible, the difficulty would remain of aggregating these different outputs. One can not add together a small furtherance of civilisation to three hundred research papers, a thousand students filtered and a multitude of scores on a variety of tests. The economists natural measure is money, and it is to attempts to use this that we now turn our consideration.

Direct Benefits: Education and Earnings

> We begin by emphasising a remarkable fact of life: between any two groups of individuals of the same age and sex, the group with more education of whatever kind will have higher average earnings from employment than the groups with less, even if the two groups are employed in the same occupational category in the same industry . . . the universality of this positive association between education and earnings (and between age and earnings) is one of the most striking findings of modern social science.[2]

Blaug's comment puts the relationship between education and earnings clearly. He mentions 'earnings' rather than 'incomes' because the latter term includes unearned incomes, such as interest or profits, and he specifies groups because it is obvious that many individuals with little education earn more than some people with a lot of education. Nevertheless the person with more education will tend to start off at a higher salary and this differential will widen as the years pass.

The evidence to substantiate these statements should ideally be drawn from longitudinal studies. That is, a representative group of people should be identified at school or before, their educational qualifications noted and their earnings throughout their career related to their education. These kinds of studies are sometimes called 'cohort' studies. Their disadvantage is obvious; they take many years of work, because the researcher has to follow the careers of the individuals, and there is the danger that by the time conclusions have been drawn initial conditions, such as the educational system or the job market, will have changed so much that the evidence will be of little value.

An alternative approach is to use cross-sectional evidence; that is, on a particular date to take a sample survey of the population asking questions about education and earnings. This approach has a number of difficulties – for instance, individuals may refuse to answer – and the validity of the exercise depends on the assumption that the experience of present day forty-year-olds, for example, will be repeated for the coming generation. Most evidence, however, on the relationship between education and earnings makes use of cross-sectional studies.

Table 3.1 presents indices of average earnings by education in ten economies, standardised so that primary education equals 100.

It should be noted that the countries are not precisely comparable, for terms such as 'primary', 'secondary' and 'higher' have different meanings in different countries and the quality of education will be different for each country. However, the picture presented by the table is clear. More education means higher earnings. More precisely, if we ignore the rather exceptional figures for Belgium, which might arise from the particular educational classification used, completion of secondary education means on average an extra 40% gain in annual earnings, whilst higher education is associated with a 77% gain over secondary education. These differentials are larger in the poorer OECD countries and this may reflect a general pattern. OECD countries are the richer countries of the world. A study of seven poorer countries suggests that in these areas completion of secondary education means on average an increase of 139% gain in earnings whilst those completing higher education will receive 167% more than those who leave school after secondary education.[3] Thus the evidence suggests that whilst on average those with more education earn more in every country, they will earn relatively much more in poor countries.

Table 3.1 *Index of Average Annual Earnings of Labour by Level of Education in OECD Countries*

Country	*Year*	*Primary*	*Educational Level* *Secondary*	*Higher*
Belgium	1960	100	251	502
Canada	1961	100	144	263
France	1968	100	183	289
Greece	1960	100	139	220
Italy	1969	100	141	244
Japan	1968	100	117	161
Netherlands	1965	100	131	152
Norway	1966	100	140	213
USA	1967	100	129	200
UK	1967	100	140	225

Source: Psacharopoulos, G., *Earnings and Education in OECD Countries*, OECD, Paris, 1975, p. 165.

The relationship between earnings and education is often presented in the form of age-earnings profiles by level of education. Typical profiles are given in Figure 3.1. Although these are hypothetical they are typical of actual profiles for most countries.

Profiles such as this illustrate a number of points. Earnings increase with age and then level off or even decline. Those with higher education show steeper rises in earnings and the higher the educational attainment the later is the year at which maximum earnings are reached and the higher are retirement earnings. Thus those with higher education have the disadvantage that they have to wait before starting to earn, but once their education is completed they earn more than the less educated and this advantage will continue and increase.

The relationship in Britain between earnings and education has been investigated by Psacharopoulos and Layard. Their analysis concentrated on nearly 7000 male employees using data for the 1972 General Household Survey. Their results confirmed the basic hypothetical picture presented in Figure 3.1 though they found one exception to the general rule that higher qualifications means higher earnings. The exception was for those with non-graduate school teaching qualifications who end up earning barely more than those with just GCE A levels. Overall they found that one extra year of schooling raises weekly earnings by about 8.5%.[4]

Figure 3.1 Typical Age-Earning Profiles

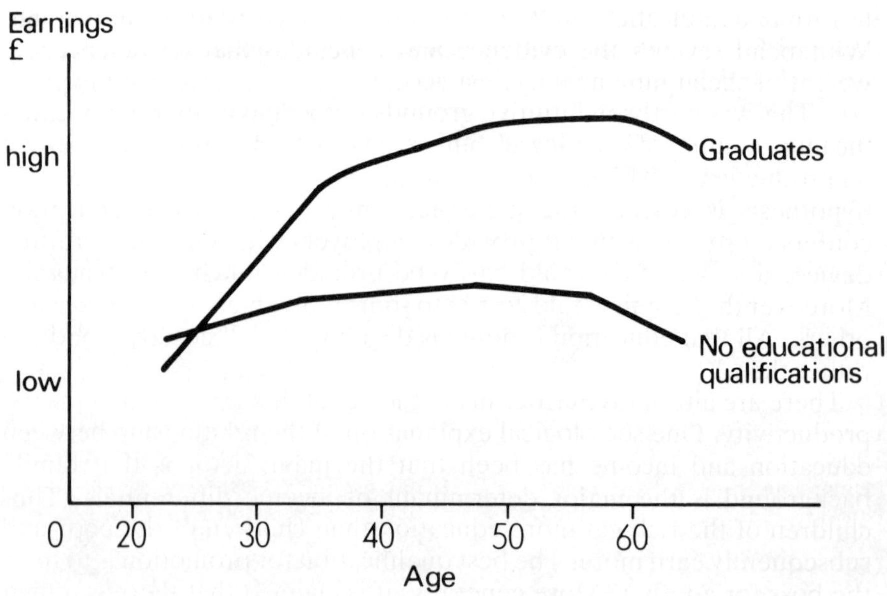

From the individual's point of view the monetary advantage of a good education is clear – what is less certain is whether society as a whole benefits from the higher earnings of individuals. The argument that it does rests on the assumption that these extra earnings are the result of higher productivity. If education causes people to be more productive, then educated people will produce more goods and services. These additional products may be enjoyed by the educated or transferred (by such measures as tax) to others. In any event higher productivity will mean that someone in society will benefit. The argument is thus about whether these higher earnings are the result of higher productivity or are caused by other factors, such as screening. This latter hypothesis suggests that educated people earn more, not because they are more productive, but because they possess qualifications such as a degree. Education thus becomes a selecting and signalling device, telling employers which candidates have ability or providing them with a rationale for selection. Thus if five candidates apply for a job and only one is a graduate, there is a fairly good chance that the graduate will be chosen. It is thus the possession of credentials which gives rise to higher earnings, not higher productivity. This argument is typified by the title of Berg's book – *Education and Jobs: the Great Training Robbery*.[5] The argument is difficult to resolve and debate has continued.[6] The strongest argument against the screening hypothesis is the evidence from internal labour markets. In other words, firms tend to promote or transfer from within rather than appoint constantly from outside. When they appoint from within it seems reasonable to assume they would pay less attention to formal qualifications and more to the track record of the individual. Whitehead reviews the evidence and concludes that on balance the weight of the argument is against acceptance of the screening hypothesis. This was partly on intuitive grounds – it would be extremely odd if the huge number of vocational courses in British education had no effect on productivity.[7] The importance of this debate is that if the screening hypothesis is correct, the main economic benefit which education confers on society is that it provides employers with a useful recruiting device, a service that could easily be provided much more cheaply. Moreover the benefit would accrue to some individuals at the expense of others. All that education is doing is deciding that *X* gets the good job rather than *Y*.

There are alternative criticisms of the belief that education improves productivity. One sociological explanation of the relationship between education and income has been that the main factor is that family background is the major determinant of income differentials. Thus children of the rich get more education than children of the poor and subsequently earn more. The best qualification for promotion is to have the boss for a father. More generally, it is claimed that there is a high correlation between parent's social class and the subsequent earnings of children. This argument is put by writers such as Bowles.[8] Clearly, family background has some effect, but the problem is to determine its precise extent. This is difficult, not only because of the problems involved in putting into operation concepts such as 'family background', but because factors such as ability, background, class, parental wealth and education are also closely linked. One exploration of the economic benefits of education is that of Fägerlind in a longitudinal study of 15000 individuals in Sweden from 1938 to 1971. His results suggest that family background exerts only a minor influence on earnings independently of education, though factors such as type of education were important.[9] However, results from one country may not be transferable to others.

A related argument is that higher earnings are not the result of education, but rather of ability. In other words, people with a lot of schooling earn more not because of this schooling but because they are clever and would have earned more in any case. The hypothesis is the subject of a large but inconclusive literature. In part, this is because the effect of ability will vary according to the course. Thus school leavers taking training as hairdressers are probably no more intelligent than those who do not take such training, and if they subsequently receive higher incomes, these are not the result of their intelligence but of their training. On the other hand people who take degrees in mathematics may well be cleverer than those who do not go into higher education, and their subsequent earnings may be due to their intelligence rather than their training. As with family background, what is at issue is not whether ability has an effect, but the extent to which earnings are due to ability.

One survey of the literature is that of Psacharopoulos. He comments that the data used in the studies leaves much to be desired because the samples tend to be small and relate to white males in the urban parts of the USA. He concludes that: 'regardless of the level of education or the ability . . . . education is responsible for over three quarters of observed earnings differentials'. Adjustment for ability alone would reduce observed earnings differentials by only 14%.[10] A less precise, more cautious review of the evidence is that of Cohn who concludes 'the truth of the matter is that no one really knows what proportion of the observed education-income relationship is strictly due to education. . . . It is doubtful if this problem will ever be solved unambiguously'.[11]

Another problem to be considered is to what extent earnings differentials are the result of monopoly power rather than productivity. From the individual's perspective this does not matter, for the question then is 'should I take this course?', and the answer will depend in part on expected earnings following from the course. Whether these arise from monopoly or from productivity is irrelevant so far as the individual considering his own interest is concerned, but crucial for society. The usual examples of monopoly in this context are groups such as lawyers, doctors and dentists, who control entry to the profession. Are their high earnings the result of productivity or because they prevent competition?

In a competitive economy employers will pay identical workers the same wages and the wage will be equal to the productivity of the worker concerned. It is clear that labour markets are not completely competitive; we are again concerned with extent. Some writers claim that this monopoly element is substantial: 'the wage system is in fact, a system of administered price, not market prices. Therefore these measurements are measuring the consequences of a process of market imperfections so serious as to invalidate the results if they are used to estimate returns to education'.[12] The hypothesis is difficult to test for we cannot assess whether monopoly income exists by simply comparing earnings in different professions. The costs of training have also to be taken into account. Moreover the position may vary in different countries, earnings reported by groups such as doctors may be less than their actual earnings, and factors such as the number of hours worked have to be considered. Psacharopoulos reviews the evidence and rather tentatively concludes that the extent of monopoly incomes may be less than is often claimed, but may exist for certain groups such as dentists or some particular medical specialisms.[13]

In general wages are more likely to reflect productivity in economies, and in those sectors of the economy, where firms are competing most strongly. They are less likely to reflect productivity in monopolistic situations or in bureaucratic institutions, such as the civil service, where productivity is impossible to measure.

To sumarise this section on education and earnings: there is a clear association between these two variables. However, the extent to which education causes higher earnings is not certain because factors such as ability and family background affect earnings. Moreover, it is not certain that higher earnings reflect higher productivity, for they may be the result of screening or of monopoly in the labour market. There is also some uncertainty as to whether society as a whole gains significantly, or whether the individual being educated gets most of the benefit.

Modification of Direct Returns

In any systematic analysis of the benefits of education, for example in completing a cost benefit analysis, the benefits need to be modified in various ways. The major modification is to take account of unemployment. The obvious reason for this is that some courses may make possible high earnings for some, yet for many people who take the course work may be difficult to obtain. Perhaps the best example of this is training for actors. To take the average earnings of working actors as a measure of the benefits of drama school would be seriously misleading as so many actors are out of work.

We can examine two main ways in which education affects unemployment patterns – the likelihood that individuals will become unemployed and the duration of unemployment. Because educated individuals are more expensive to hire and fire, and possess skills which are specific to the firm, we might expect them to have less probability of becoming unemployed; however once unemployed these factors may mean that the duration of unemployment is fairly similar to those with less education. American evidence supports these expectations.[14] In Britain Nickell analysed data from over 7000 males and concluded that each year of schooling up to twelve years reduces the probability of entering unemployment at any age by 25%, and also reduces the expected duration of unemployment by just over 4%. Possession of qualifications of O level or above reduces the chances of becoming unemployed to just over one third of the no qualification level and also reduces expected duration by 12%.[15] It is not certain however that skill *creates* jobs. As Vaizey points out, if the number of employment opportunities is limited, giving extra training to some of the unemployed may mean that these obtain work, but it will be at the expense of other, less skilled workers who do not get the jobs. There is a reshuffle in which one group of unemployed persons are substituted for other unemployed persons.[16]

Thus for the individual, extended education not only increases earnings, but it also reduces the likelihood of unemployment and to a smaller extent its duration. There may also be a more general effect if there is an imbalance in the economy with employers finding difficulty in appointing skilled people. If these posts could be filled then jobs dependant on them but requiring less skill may also be created. A variation on this is the 'great people' argument. To the extent that education enables great inventors to achieve their potential, it may lead to the creation of thousands of jobs.

A related point concerns not unemployment as such, but rather participation in the labour force. This is particularly important in the case of women, as better educated women are more likely to go out to work.[17] The economic explanation for this is that education raises women's productivity in the labour market thus raising the opportunity cost if they stay at home.[18]

The direct returns to education must also be modified to take account of mortality. This reduces the returns to education because some individuals die during their working life and are therefore no longer productive. For large groups the effect is slight, though of considerable importance to the individuals concerned.

Adjustments must also be made to take account of taxes, though this is not necessary when the perspective is that of society because the economist is concerned with real resources; taxes merely represent a transfer of money from one group to another. They do not represent a general increase or decrease in resources. For the individual however taxes are certainly relevant and calculations of benefit are made net of taxes. This tends to reduce the private returns to education, because educated individuals have higher earnings and these attract higher rates of tax.

Indirect Monetary Benefits

Education also creates indirect monetary benefits. One example of this is that there is a relationship between the amount of education an individual receives and subsequent training.[19] This may be because firms tend to invest more in workers who have received a lot of schooling, as these can add to their productivity more easily and cheaply, since any specific training can rest on the foundation of the general education. Post school training gives rise to various benefits, just as general education does. The most obvious of these is that of higher earnings, but most of the benefits discussed here as resulting from general education also apply to training.[20] These benefits may accrue to the individual or to society, for example in the form of higher production, whilst the cost of the training may be paid by the individual, the firm or society or be shared by all three.

This relationship between education and training is in fact a specific example of what is sometimes called 'the option value of education'. In other words, completion of one stage of education gives rise to the option of completing other stages. Thus a student who completes GCE A level may well acquire the possibility of entering a degree course; a student completing a degree course may then have the opportunity of entering a specific training for a particular career. There is no double counting here. The situation is rather like a customer buying a machine and in doing so acquiring the right to a subsequent machine at a discount. The analogy is not precise, for the option value of an education has no market value as it cannot be sold, whereas the option to buy a machine may be transferable. However it does have a value, though this will vary from individual to individual and many may not choose to exercise their option.

Some of these indirect benefits do not accrue to the individual being educated but to others, in particular to other members of his family. A clear example of this arises from early childhood education. If young children go to school, they are receiving not only an education but a child care service which frees the parents, usually the mother, for other activities. This is particularly true when the youngest child goes to school; the benefit is less obvious if there are still younger children to be looked after. This benefit is partly financial, in that it allows both parents to look for work and so increase their incomes, which also benefits society as a whole, since it increases total national income. This kind of non-direct financial benefit may well cover a large part of the costs of early schooling. In the USA Weisbrod undertook a rough-and-ready calculation which suggested that the value to society of the child care services of elementary schools was sufficient to cover a quarter of the total resource costs of the schools (that is excluding capital outlays but including implicit interest and depreciation). The total child care value was actually greater than this, as the calculation disregards the benefits to parents who do not work.[21] Whilst very approximate, this kind of approach suggests that there is a substantial argument for expanding nursery education which is usually ignored. The effect will vary over time and between societies; for example, if unemployment rates are high, many parents will be unable to obtain employment when their children go to school and there will be no direct financial benefit for them. There may well be a substantial non-financial benefit in that parents have much more free time to devote to other activities. An indication of the importance of this is the eagerness with which many parents look forward to their child's entry to school and to the end of the school holidays!

Some of the indirect benefits make their presence felt much later. An inter-generation effect arises because there is a link between the education of parents and the education of children. Thus the Robbins committee on Higher Education showed that if the father's education had extended to the age of 18 or over there was a 32% chance that the child would enter full time higher education. If the father had left school under 16 the child had only a 2% probability of entering higher education. Very similar links obtained between the education of mother and child.[22] Such evidence as this shows a strong correlation between the education of parent and child, but it does not prove cause and effect, because other factors such as social class, family size and intelligence are also linked to education of parent and child and it is difficult to separate out these influences. Nevertheless, there is evidence to suggest that whilst these may be important, parent's education does affect the child's attainment.[23] This is not really surprising. An obvious way in which this comes about is that parents help their children with homework; clearly more educated parents can give more help. The influence is more pervasive than this, however. As women become more educated and more likely to be employed, it might be assumed that they will spend less time on the care of the children. The evidence does not support this. Educated mothers tend to spend less time on general household activities, such as meal preparation and laundry, but more time on child care activities than do less educated women. Alexander surveys a number of studies which suggest that children of the better educated have more total time spent on them by adults than do the children of the less well educated, perhaps because the former have a greater time preference for the future, and are more willing to invest their time now to obtain future benefits for their children. Inter-generational transfer of knowledge is therefore much more pronounced among educated household.[24] Education may also affect the size of the family.

Cochrane's summary of the evidence suggests that in poor countries education increases the ability to have live births, probably because of improved health and nutrition. In societies with improved levels of female literacy, education lowers the demand for children by altering their perceived costs and benefits, and it enables couples to limit their fertility more efficiently through more access to contraceptive knowledge.[25]

There are a number of other indirect financial returns to education, largely arising because educated individuals extend their competence in a number of areas. The usual example of this in the literature is the rather odd one of being able to complete an income tax return, and therefore having no need to employ an accountant. There are other examples which could be given – a greater ability to claim social security benefits; to obtain extra freelance work, such as evening class teaching or part-time journalism, to assemble a hi-fi system or to become a more efficient consumer. Moreover, as Alexander puts it 'a more highly educated individual will possess a certain economic serendipity which affects his economic choices'.

Some of the indirect benefits accrue to the individual and some to society as a whole. The ability to claim legitimate social security benefits confers no benefit to society; the ability to complete a tax form may create general benefits because it means that society can use tax systems, which would not be possible if most people could not complete the forms. This is in fact a specific example of a general case: that literate societies can use superior forms of administration. Even if it is possible to determine where the benefit lies, most of these indirect benefits are impossible to measure; indeed it is usually not even possible to say if the benefits are large or small.

Non-Monetary Returns

The distinction between money and non-money benefits can only be approximate, for the individual or group receiving the benefit may in fact have a choice as to how the benefit is received. However, what are usually called 'consumption benefits' are usually non-monetary. They are given this name to distinguish them from investment, though the distinction is not precise. For most purposes it is sufficient that investment goods are usually those which are used to produce other benefits in the future. Thus a weaving loom is clearly an investment good as it is used to produce cloth. Consumer goods or services are those which give or aim to give satisfaction to consumers; ice cream, a visit to the zoo and flowers in the garden are all consumption goods. Education is both an investment and a consumption good. It is investment because it makes possible higher production and benefits in the future; it is consumption because it gives satisfaction now. If the population of a country believes that education is desirable in its own right and is willing to pay additional taxes for this purpose, then the value of education as consumption ought to be added to its value as an investment, even though the benefit goes primarily to the individuals who are educated rather than to society as a whole.

Consumption benefits accruing to education have a number of peculiarities which do not apply to non-educational benefits. For example, educational benefits are often spread over many years; the benefit of an ice cream or a zoo visit may not last long, though, like Wordsworth's daffodils, some non-educational benefits are long lasting.

We may divide the educational benefits into two main groups: those relating to work and those to leisure, though in some cases there is overlap. After university a former student may receive prestige or status which give satisfaction at work or at leisure. This is also one reason for the prevalence of the old school tie. Another example of this overlap is that there is some evidence that educated people have better health.[26] This in turn would affect both work and leisure.

The nature and value of these leisure related consumption benefits are uncertain. In so far as education increases the student's ability to satisfy given expectations and tasks it is an undoubted benefit, but education also changes tastes and values and this makes comparison difficult. How can we determine what pleasure a person might have got out of life if he had not been to college? Part of the result of an education is that the range of choice of activities widens. One characteristic of colleges is their wide variety of clubs and societies ranging from archery to zoology. Attendance at such events makes it possible for students to acquire new interests which may give pleasure for years. Moreover, existing interests may be developed and expanded, giving rise to deeper understanding, though as Peacock and Wiseman point out, a man who has always enjoyed Beethoven does not necessarily enhance his pleasure by taking a course in musical appreciation.[27] This problem is impossible to solve since there is no way accurately to compare enjoyment before and after the course. Moreover there is no reason to suppose that any information we obtain about one person would apply to others.

Leisure related consumption benefits may in fact be non-existent, or even negative in that education may change tastes and activities. 'I used to like. . . .' may be the lament of the graduate, looking back to a cheerful childhood which existed before education made him too sophisticated to enjoy simple pleasures. The argument is not so much that ignorance is bliss but that pleasures lost in acquiring an education, might be stronger than the newly acquired ones. Clearly the situation will vary with the individual, and no definite conclusion can be confidently stated.

Work related consumption benefits can be analysed in a number of ways. In the short run a student's 'work' is as a student. The consumption satisfaction obtained from this will differ from individual to individual, but the measure required is the opportunity cost of what is given up. The youngster playing truant or 'creeping unwillingly to school' shows that for some children these benefits are zero or negative. On the other hand 'schooldays are the happiest days', whilst over-dramatic, does illustrate that for many people school is better than the alternative. This is even more likely to be true at college where attendance is voluntary. Whatever the disadvantages of undergraduate life, for many students it is clearly much better than working. Whilst the benefit cannot be quantified, it is clearly substantial.

This kind of consumption benefit frequently extends into later working life so that educated people receive various non-pecuniary benefits. One way in which these occur is as fringe benefits; that is goods or services paid for by the employer but received by the individual. These fringe benefits include medical insurance, pension plans, subsidised meals, company cars and so on. Another area relates to working conditions such as the health and safety of the job, the degree of work autonomy and the physical comfort of the working conditions. Moreover many professional people obtain considerable enjoyment from their work. Thus a sample of British university teachers rated their work as better than the most likely alternative in such aspects as holidays, in the intrinsic interest of the job and in allowing them freedom to organise their working methods.[28]

From an economic analysis perspective it is not sufficient to agree that such non-pecuniary benefits exist; it is necessary to show that they derive from education and if possible to measure them. Casual observation would tend to support the hypothesis that educated people tend to obtain jobs with better non-pecuniary benefits. Some statistical support for this association was obtained by Duncan using a Quality of Employment Survey in the USA. Duncan found that the relationship between education and his variables was 'dramatic and unambiguous'.[29] Despite this work it is not possible to measure precisely such benefits as 'satisfaction' and the evidence remains strong but unquantifiable.

This is a limitation of most work done on the returns to education, particularly because some jobs held by educated workers may have substantial non-pecuniary advantages, and therefore pay less than other jobs. These benefits go to the individual and are usually considered as private benefits, though there is some discussion as to whether they should be counted as an advantage to society. If the aim is economic growth, then these consumptive benefits should not be counted, because they do not lead to growth. However if policy aims at the maximum welfare of the people, including psychic as well as financial satisfactions, then these consumption benefits should be counted as accruing to society as well as to the individual.

External Benefits

The Robbins Report suggested that the return on investment in education could not be measured completely in terms such as the above. 'There is a further return in the shape of general adaptability and increased technological advance which in the last analysis is probably more important than what is measured within the system of relative prices'.[30]

This notion of external effects is an important one in many areas of economics. They exist when the activities of one firm or individual have a direct effect on others as opposed to an indirect effect, as they would through the price system. Thus an externality arises when a house extension affects the light available to a neighbour, or when a firm throws its waste into a river affecting those downstream.

The concept of externalities is a broad one; indeed it is difficult to know where to draw the line. Almost any action of one individual can affect other people. If I smoke, this discomforts others; if I write a reference for one person, it may affect others who would like the job; if my garden is attractive, then passers-by benefit. These spillover effects are not only extensive, they are difficult to categorise let alone measure. Thus researchers have studied the effects of education on the size of family and the efficient use of contraceptives, on political attitudes, on the propensity to save and on consumer decisions.[31] Whilst many studies such as these are useful and informative, reading the literature in this area can lead one to speculate that it may be more profitable to assess what is not affected by education!

A good illustration of the difficulties involved in this area is afforded by the many studies of the relationship between education and crime. A number of writers have suggested that one effect of education is that it reduces crime. Thus Ehrlich, using American data, shows that juveniles not in school show much higher delinquency rates than those enrolled in school, and he provides arguments to suggest that higher education enhances law enforcement.[32] Alexander quotes other research to show that education reduces crime primarily because it reduces unemployment, and the employed commit fewer crimes. A rise in family income is associated with lower crime; as education raises income it is logical to suppose that education reduces crime. Prisoners have lower educational attainments than the average person and much higher illiteracy rates. Moreover a survey of riot participants found that inadequate education and lower levels of employment were among the top four grievances which motivated disorders.[33] As West shows, these kinds of argument have a long history, but must be looked at with a good deal of scepticism.[34] Firstly there are all kinds of problems concerned with the definition of 'crime'. Should we include such activities as riding a bicycle without lights or playing football in the streets? Then there are problems concerning statistics. Educated people may be less likely to be caught, or their education may make them more skilled in getting off, or they may commit different kinds of crime, such as fraud, which are less likely to be detected or prosecuted. But these problems are minor compared to the nature of the evidence. Almost all the studies which support the view that education lowers crime use correlational evidence. Whatever their apparent statistical sophistication this usually amounts to little more than a measure that the two are linked. They do not show causation. There may well be a distributional element here. Those with more education may obtain satisfactory economic rewards without resorting to crime; the extension of education may not extend these rewards to others. Since there will never be equality of educational achievement, there will always be some relatively deprived who may resort to crime to achieve adequate reward – and these may not necessarily be financial but include non-material rewards such as excitement or status. Correlation evidence can be a double-edged sword. In almost every country the last few decades have seen an extension of education and the growth of crime. Thus facile claims that one benefit of education is that it reduces crime must be treated as little more than idle speculation.

A related claim made for education is that it affects behaviour more generally, for one aim of any education system is that it attempts to inculcate acceptable social values in children. In a denominational school the prime purpose of the school would fall into this area. More generally, education is, as Durkheim observed 'above all the means by which society perpetually recreates the conditions of its very existence'.[35] By passing established beliefs, knowledge and values from one generation to another, education contributes to continuity and the persistence of an organised social life. This function can be most clearly observed in countries other than one's own, for familiarity sometimes prevents keen analysis. In the USA, particularly around the turn of the century, the schools played a key role in Americanising the mass of immigrants. A similar process can be seen in many African countries today, where the schools are concerned to reinforce the national identity and flag-raising ceremonies, marching, pledges of allegiance and singing the national anthem are merely the visible signs of more widespread but subtler processes. This socialisation is not just present at particular times and places, but is an all pervasive, though usually unacknowledged, purpose of education. Despite its importance, it is often ignored by those assessing the output of education because it is impossible to quantify.

A specific example of this general socialisation function is the effect education has on political life. There seems to be some kind of association between the level of education in a country and the presence of democracy, though clearly there are many exceptions to this correlation. Education may strengthen democracy, because it is easier to control and mislead ignorant people. Thus at one time it was a criminal act in the USA to teach slaves to read. The educated mind is liable to question and to argue. Weisbrod shows that educated people are more likely to vote, to be active members of political organisations, to attend political meetings, are more informed about political issues and are more anxious to see that other people become informed.[36] Again this is correlational evidence and must be viewed cautiously, but the argument is plausible. If education does play a significant part in the development and maintenance of democracy it is a benefit of enormous importance though impossible to quantify.

There are more localised externalities. Siting a college or university in a particular locality benefits the area not only because it creates jobs, but because it offers facilities to local people, such as attendance at lectures or concerts, use of the library and sponsorship of civic events. Just as educated people are more likely to be active politically, they may also participate more fully in non-political civic activities such as theatre groups, preserving old buildings, archaeological digs or running local music societies. However it is not clear to what extent these activities benefit society generally, as opposed to a select group of educated people. If they are limited then these ought to be considered the private benefits of the educated sections of society.

The external 'outputs' discussed in this section are so broad and diffuse that they cannot be measured and this has led a number of economists to play down their importance. This may lead to the simple error of assuming that what can't be measured can be ignored.

Economic 'bads'

So far this chapter has discussed the outputs of education as if they were almost entirely beneficial. This is obviously not the whole story. Those who live adjacent to bus stops used by local secondary school pupils will doubtless be aware of disadvantages arising from mass education.

There are a number of critics of the effects of the present system of education. One group are the 'de-schoolers' whose principal spokesman is Ivan Illich. They see the educational system itself as essentially harmful. In their opinion, schools are strongholds of privilege, encourage authoritarianism, cause middle class children to become passive inmates playing the system and reject working class children who drop out and are labelled as failures. Schools are seen as model bureaucracies geared towards the indoctrination of docile consumers and should be abolished and replaced by alternatives where education would be encouraged in non-formal, open access centres.[37]

Earlier in the chapter it was pointed out that education may change tastes rather than extend them. This effect may be wider than was then suggested. Jane Austen commented with some tartness on schools 'where young ladies for enormous pay might be screwed out of health and into vanity'.[38] Whilst the cost may have changed, the result still continues. Graduates hope for 'good' jobs and find that employment opportunities are limited. The ensuing frustration could more than offset many of the benefits. It has often been recognised that student unrest may disturb societies, and this may be particularly important in developing countries where, as Balogh and Streeten point out, unemployed intellectuals create political instability and encourage value systems which disparage physical labour.[39]

In recent years the notion of 'over-education' has gained popularity. Though the term is associated with a variety of meanings, in essence it suggests that too much education is being produced relative to what is necessary or efficient. One effect of this is that expectations are not fulfilled. Rumberger quotes evidence which suggests that considerable numbers of American college graduates earn substantially less than they expected.[40] He concludes that over-education is widespread and will continue as long as those with more schooling fare better in the labour-market than those with less. One result is that individuals will continue to compete for the really good jobs in the economy, blaming only themselves if they fail to acquire them.[41]

The notion of over-education is widely accepted by Marxist critics. Carnoy and Levin claim that the legitimacy of schooling as both a selection device for jobs and as an agent of social mobility requires a constant expansion of enrolments in order to absorb the social demand for increases in educational attainments. There has not been a corresponding increase in opportunities, so that recently educated workers are increasingly difficult to integrate into the traditional wage-labour system. This leads to 'increasing problems of worker turnover, absenteeism, sabotage, wildcat strikes and slowdowns, drugs and alcoholism'.[42] This group of critics see the education system as an institution which serves to perpetuate the social relationships of economic life by facilitating the integration of youth into the labour force. Schools achieve this by fostering legitimate inequality through the meritocratic manner in which they regard students. They create and reward certain patterns of social class, racial and sexual identification, and foster types of personal development (e.g., traits such as submission to authority) compatible with the relationship needed at work. Finally schools create surpluses of skilled labour which benefit employers.[43] These characteristics are not limited to the school situation, but also apply to lifelong education, where the principal beneficiaries are the skilled workers, supervisors and management at the expense of groups such as women and immigrants.[44]

Whatever the precise merits of this line of argument, it is clear that the output of education is not necessarily always beneficial, and these 'bads' ought to be kept in mind when considering the relative costs and benefits.

References

1 Wagner., L., 'The Measurement of Output' in *The Internal Efficiency of Educational Institutions*, Open University Course ED 322, 1977.
2 Blaug, M., *Education and the Employment Problems in Developing Countries*, International Labour Office, 1973, p. 27.
3 Psacharopoulos, G., *Returns to Education: An International Comparison*, Elsevier, 1973, p. 132.
4 Psacharopoulos, G. and Layard, R., 'Human Capital and Earnings: British Evidence and a Critique' *Review of Economic Studies*, Vol. XLVI No. 3, July 1979, pp. 485–504.
5 Berg, I., *Education and Jobs: the Great Training Robbery*, Beacon Press, 1971.
6 *see for example* Wise, O. A., 'Academic Achievement and Job Performance' *American Economic Review*, Vol. 65 No. 3, June 1973, pp. 350–65 or Goodman, J. D., 'The Economic Returns to Education: An Assessment of Alternative Models' *Social Science Quarterly*, Vol. 60 No. 2, September 1979, pp. 269–83.
7 Whitehead, A. K., 'Screening and Education: A Theoretical and Empirical Study' *British Review of Economic Issues*, Vol. 3 No. 8, Spring 1981, pp. 884–62.
8 Bowles, S., 'Schooling and Equality from Generation to Generation' *Journal of Political Economy*, Vol. 80, May/June 1972, pp. 219–51.
9 Fagerlind, I., *Formal Education and Adult Earnings*, Almquist & Wicksell, Stockholm, 1975.
10 Psacharopoulos, G., *Earnings and Education in OECD Countries*, OECD Paris, 1975, pp. 54–5.
11 Cohn, E., *The Economics of Education*, revised ed., 1979, p. 47.
12 Vaizey, J., *Economics of Education*, Faber & Faber, 1962, p. 45.
13 Psacharopoulos, G., *Earnings and Education in OECD Countries*, *op. cit.*, Ch. 5.
14 Ashenfelter, O. and Ham, J., 'Education Unemployment and Earnings' *Journal of Political Economy*, Vol. 87 No. 5 Pt 2, 1979, pp. §99–§115.
15 Nickell, S., 'Education and Lifetime Patterns of Unemployment' *Journal of Political Economy*, Vol. 87 No. 5 Pt 2, 1979, pp. §117–§131.
16 Vaizey, J., 'The School in Question: an Economist's Viewpoint' *Oxford Review of Education*, Vol. 5 No. 3, October 1979, pp. 207–14.
17 Woodhall, M., 'The Economic Returns to Investment in Women's Education' *Higher Education*, Vol. 2, 1973, pp. 275–300 and Leibowitz, A., 'Education and the Allocation of Women's Time' in Juster, F. J., ed., *Education Income and Human Behaviour*, McGraw-Hill, 1975.
18 Alexander, K., 'The Value of an Education' *Journal of Educational Finance*, Vol. 1. No. 4, Spring 1976, pp. 429–67.
19 Mincer, J., 'On the job training: Costs, Returns and Some Implications' *Journal of Political Economy*, Vol. LXX Pt 2, October 1962, pp. 50–70, and Psacharopoulos, E. and Layard, R., *op. cit.*
20 Drake, K., *The Cost Effectiveness of Vocational Training: A Survey of British Studies*, mimeograph, Manchester University, 1979.
21 Weisbrod, B. A., *External Benefits of Public Education*, Princeton, 1964, p. 29.

22 *Report of the Committee on Higher Education* (Robbins), HMSO, 1963, Appendix 1, p. 60.
23 Davie, R., Butler, N. and Goldstein, H., *From Birth to Seven*, Longman, 1972, p. 36f.
24 Alexander, K., *op. cit.*
25 Cochrane, S. H., *Fertility and Education*, Johns Hopkins University Press, 1979, p. 10.
26 Lefcowitz, M. J., 'Poverty and Health: a re-examination' *Inquiry*, March 1973, pp. 3–13.
27 Peacock, A. and Wiseman, J., 'Principles of Educational Finance in Developed Countries' in Blaug, M., ed., *Economics of Education 2*, Penguin, 1969.
28 Williams, G., Blackstone, T. and Metcalf, D., *The Academic Labour Market*, Elsevier, 1974, Ch. 11.
29 Duncan, G. J., 'Earnings Functions and Non-Pecuniary Benefits' *Journal of Human Resources*, Vol. xi No. 4, Fall 1976, pp. 462–83.
30 *Report of the Committee on Higher Education, op. cit.*
31 *See for example* Juster, E. T., ed., *Education, Income and Human Behaviour*, McGraw-Hill, 1975, Ch. 1.
32 Ehrlich, I., 'On the relationship between Education and Crime', in Juster, F. T., ed., *op. cit.*
33 Alexander, K., *op. cit.*
34 West, E. G., *Education and the State*, Institute of Economic Affairs, 2nd ed., 1970, Ch. 3.
35 Durkheim, E., *Education and Sociology*, trans. S. O., Fox, Free Press, 1956, p. 123.
36 Weisbrod, B. A., *op. cit.* Ch. 8.
37 Illich, I., *De-schooling Society*, Caldar & Boyars, 1971.
38 Austen, Jane, *Emma*, Collins, 1952 ed., p. 31.
39 Balogh, T. and Streeten, P. P., 'The Planning of Education in Poor Countries', in Blaug, M., ed., *Economics of Education 1*, Penguin, 1968.
40 Rumberger, R. W., *Overeducation in the US Labour Market*, Praeger, 1981, p. 6.
41 *ibid.*, p. 127.
42 Carnoy, M. and Levin, H. M., *The Limits of Educational Reform*, David McKay, 1976, p. 11.
43 Bowles, S. and Gintis, H., 'Economic Analysis of Lifelong Education', in Dave, R. H., ed., *Foundations of Lifelong Education*, Pergamon Press for UNESCO, 1976, p. 324.
44 Vinokur, A., 'Economic Analysis of Lifelong Education' in Dave, R. H., ed., *op. cit.*, p. 324.

4

Education and Economic Growth

Measurement

The conventional way to measure economic growth is to use estimates of the national income. This can be done by comparing total national income in one year with that in another and calculating the percentage change after making allowance for inflation. A refinement of this method is to divide the total national income by the population to obtain a figure per head. Thus in 1982 national income in the UK was around £200 000, the total population was about 55 million and so per capita national income was roughly £3600. After allowing for inflation, this figure can be compared to earlier or later years to obtain a measure of growth.

However these measures of growth have a number of weaknesses. Firstly the figures always contain a number of inaccuracies because it is difficult to measure something as complex as the total income of a country. This is compounded when comparisons are made over a long period because adjustments to allow for inflation are less accurate. It is easier to measure inflation between 1980 and 1981 than between 1950 and 1980.

Even where the figures are accurate, what they measure is limited, for they only apply to what is called the 'market economy', so that only work that is paid for is included. This means that the value of housework for example is ignored. Moreover the figures make no allowance for changes in quality. If colour televisions, calculators or cars become more or less efficient, this will not show in the figures. If we spend more on tanks and less on education or health this might show as a rise in national income, but the quality of life would be lower. Similarly the figures ignore external effects: if more cigarettes are smoked this will be reflected in a rise of national income, but the loss of welfare of non-smokers in smoke-filled rooms will be ignored. So national income figures do not measure welfare or the quality of life; they merely estimate the total of goods and services available to a country over the year.

These limitations have led a number of writers to suggest alternative measures. Thus Harbison asks if income maximisation should be the primary measure of development and suggests three possible alternatives.[1] One of these is an index of educational development which combines secondary enrolment ratios and higher education ratios weighted by a factor of five. It thus measures 'schooling capacity'. An alternative to this is an index of nutrition which attempts to measure both the quantity and the quality of food consumed. Harbison's other alternative is an indicator of health by using figures for life expectancy at birth. These alternatives have a number of limitations; in particular they are partial measures in that they attempt to measure only particular aspects of life, and the data used to construct them is frequently very unreliable. Examination of these indicators shows that they are significantly correlated, but that in many cases this correlation is not close, as some countries do better on one measure than another.

It would be quite possible to develop other indicators, such as data for infant mortality or literacy, but there are always plausible alternative measures of welfare, such as housing or employment, which could be added. Also the data are often inaccurate and there are problems in combining together separate indicators.

Thus the alternatives to national income may have merit in enabling comparisons to be made in particular areas, but they are unsatisfactory as measures of growth, and national income statistics continue to be the least unsatisfactory method of measurement.

Arguments For and Against Growth

The advantages of growth are sometimes taken as self-evident, but in recent years increasing attention has been paid to the disadvantages of growth. Unless great care is taken, growth is associated with increased pollution, unspoiled countryside is replaced by factories and offices, entire species of plants and animals are wiped out for ever. As Mishan points out, there are close links between rapid economic development and many of the unpleasanter features of our civilisation. Writing about economists he comments that 'glancing at the irresistible spread of steel and concrete, at the plague of motorized traffic, at the growing impatience and tenseness of people, his thoughts may catch at a deeper apprehension of reality'.[2] For economic growth does not mean just more of the same things; it involves change, and not only change in material things. Rapid growth involves considerable adjustments to the way things are done, and consequently established ideas and beliefs are challenged. 'Things fall apart; the centre cannot hold' is the cry of one who recognises the advantages of stability. In growth, the virtues of accumulation replace those of giving. Innovation leaves behind not only obsolete machines but also workers who feel that they have become obsolete. Moreover many of the advantages of growth may prove illusory. To possess a car when few others do gives one the freedom of the road; if others also possess cars this disappears. The house on the top of the hill or the cottage in the Dordogne may lose their advantage when surrounded by others. The benefits of increased wealth are in part a relative matter: if everyone becomes better off, some of the advantages of being better off disappear.

Even in poor countries there are critics of too much emphasis on growth as an objective. A number of writers have suggested instead a 'basic needs' approach, which is seen as a more direct attack on poverty and where particular attention is given to health, nutrition and basic education. Essentially the basic needs approach shifts attention away from the goal of output maximisation to that of minimising poverty, though there is evidence that countries which do well on basic needs also have relatively high growth rates.[3]

Despite the critics, there are undoubted benefits resulting from growth. The primary reason for desiring growth is to raise the general living standards of the population. It is the most powerful weapon against poverty, for whilst redistribution of income or wealth can reduce relative poverty the absolute effects of growth are substantial. A country whose living standards grow at 3% a year will double its GNP in less than twenty five years; at 5% a year the doubling of living standards takes less than fourteen years.

Economic growth makes the redistribution of income much easier. Without growth those who are richer will try to maintain their wealth; if income is growing it is possible (at least in theory) to maintain the wealth of the better off and redistribute the growth to the poor. It is much easier for a growing economy to be generous to the poor than it is for a static one.

There may be limits to growth. As ecologists have pointed out, the earth's supply of raw materials is limited. This is particularly true of fossil fuels and basic minerals, for these are used much more extravagantly in rich countries than in poor, and the problem is intensified by the rapid rise in world population. However doomsday predictions have been made before; if there is one thing that is certain about growth, it is that it will be different in the future to what it was in the past. Future growth may involve different or fewer resources and this process will be encouraged by rapid price rises of those resources in short supply.

What Causes Growth?

The factors affecting economic growth are so varied and so interrelated, that it is not surprising that there is no full understanding of them. However, it is possible to isolate certain points which affect growth.

The quantity of labour clearly affects the opportunities for an economy to develop. Not all the people in a country are available for work; the old and the young may not be able to work and there may be influences which restrict women's participation in the labour market. Thus a country with an ageing population will find it more difficult to grow than one which has an increasing number of young people of working age. These variables can be influenced by government policy; thus during the world wars output grew partly because large numbers of women went out to work. Note that if there is no change in techniques or resources available, continued increases in the labour force will bring diminishing returns. Ten workers with two tractors may not produce any more than five workers with two tractors.

Thus quantity of capital per worker is important. This is such an important point that other causes of growth are sometimes ignored. The quantity of capital per worker depends on many factors, for example on the opportunities for investment. Workers in Saudi Arabia had very little capital per head until the discovery of oil created enormous investment opportunities. Government policies also affect the amount of investment, and one of the unsolved problems of British (and other) economic policy is how to encourage businesses to invest more.

New knowledge and inventions can make a great contribution to the growth of an economy. This is most obvious when the invention takes the form of a physical object, such as a steam engine or an internal combustion engine, but it is also important in other areas, such as better management. Political, legal and social institutions have a profound effect on economic growth, because they provide the framework in which more concrete factors, such as the quantity of labour, operate. Clearly if a country is subject to violent political upheavals, the confiscation of property, or internal warfare, it is unlikely that long term investments will be undertaken. But the argument goes deeper. Some types of land tenure system, for example, may inhibit production. If a tenant farmer has to give half his crop to the landlord, his incentive to produce more will be reduced. Religious and other beliefs also have a strong influence on growth. If these inculcate acceptance of the status quo, of a belief that man's powers to alter his situation are limited, then growth is unlikely. If religion fosters the belief that change is good, that wealth accumulation should be encouraged, then growth is more likely. Max Weber argued that the 'Protestant ethic', which laid great emphasis on hard work and wealth acquisition, was an important cause of the industrial revolution. An example may illustrate this point. For many centuries China has had good natural resources, a hard working people, a literate elite, a capacity for invention (e.g., gunpowder) but the country remained poor. There were doubtless many reasons for this, but two significant causes may have been that the scholars were not interested in the technological implications of their knowledge, and that money makers had a low status.[4]

The final factor to be discussed in this short survey is the quality of labour. 'Labour' is sometimes talked about as if it were a uniform input, but clearly there are vast differences between people. The contribution of education to economic growth seems to lie most clearly in this area. The last chapter discussed at some length the output of education and many of these outputs would contribute directly to the quality of labour. The influence is also more diffuse, for education will affect belief systems, the likelihood of innovation and the growth of knowledge, all of which influence growth.

In an analysis of the contribution of education to development, the World Bank suggested that education makes a contribution in three significant and interrelated ways. It gives people a base of knowledge, attitudes, values and skills which equip them with the potential to learn and to respond to new opportunities. Secondly, education contributes as an instrument to support programmes designed to meet other basic needs such as adequate nutrition or shelter. Finally education is seen as the development that sustains and accelerates overall development by training skilled workers, in facilitating the advancement of knowledge and in enabling the individual to identify with his changing culture and find a constructive role in society. Note that this view of the contribution of education relates to a very broad view of 'development', which could be contrasted with a narrower analysis of 'growth' limited to economic aspects.[5]

Difficulties arise if we try to be precise about the influence of education, for it is a very diverse activity, and whilst physical capital has an independent existence which makes its effects relatively easy to measure, 'human capital' is embodied in members of the labour force. Thus the return on human capital is mixed in with the return on the quantity of labour and is difficult to isolate. Nevertheless attempts have been made to analyse the contribution of education to economic growth in a number of ways.

The Residual Approach

One of the most important techniques is to make use of an aggregate *production function*. The assumption behind production functions is that it is possible to specify the relationship between what goes into the productive process and what comes out. Thus the level of output of a furniture factory depends on the input of such factors as the quantity of labour and the amount of machinery. For the economy as a whole there are various ways to analyse the relationships, but the most usual approach would be to suggest that growth in output (Q) is a function of the growth of inputs of Labour (L) and capital (K) plus an unknown *residual* or *error term* (R). Thus the basic equation is:

$$Q = f(L, K, R)$$

The residual item is needed because investigations typically find that the growth in output is greater than the increases in labour and capital in the economy. For example researchers might study the economy of a country over thirty or forty years and find that the number of hours worked increased on average by 0.5%, the amount of capital equipment increased by 1.5% but output increased by 3%. The problem thus arises as to what causes the difference between the rise in input and the consequential rise in output. One of the major researchers in this area is Schultz who analysed data for the USA between 1929 and 1957.[6] His basic method was to calculate 'the total value of the stock of education' in the two years and thus obtain a figure for the increase in this stock. He then made estimates of the rate of return on the investment in education and combines the calculations to give a figure for the growth in national income from schooling. His results suggest that between 16.5% and 20% of the total growth in the American economy was caused by the additional schooling of the labour force.

There are a number of objections to this approach. Firstly the original data is too meagre to justify confidence in the findings. Moreover the results are far too dependant on the choice of years. Finally Schultz's approach assumes that increases in income earned by the more educated compared to those with less schooling reflect real changes in production.

The most complete analysis of the sources of economic growth and of education's contribution to it, has been made by Denison in a number of books.[7] He suggests that growth in the USA had been due to five main types of change:

1 Advances in knowledge, particularly the advance in technological, managerial and organisational knowledge. Approximately a third of the growth in the US economy in the period 1929–1969 was due to advances in knowledge. This estimate is a residual because there is no way to estimate it directly.
2 Amount of work done. This accounted for almost 29% of the growth. A feature of this period was the entry of a large number of females into the labour force.
3 Capital accounted for nearly 19% of growth in the period 1929–1969. 'Capital' includes items such as non residential structures and equipment, dwellings and business inventories.
4 Education in the form of the average amount of education held by workers employed in the business sector was the source of 14% of the growth. This manifested itself in the form of increased skills and versatility.
5 Improved resource allocation, for example labourers transferring

from relatively unproductive farming to industry, accounted for 10% of the growth.

Denison's method is quite complex and involves very detailed investigation of the national income accounts, but it is possible to give a very brief (and possibly grossly oversimplified) account of the way he estimates the effect of education. There are two basic steps; the first is to calculate an index of educational inputs in the economy. He does this by giving weights to various levels of education (e.g. no schooling = 75, eight years schooling = 100, five or more years of college = 219). He adjusts these numbers to take account of the participation in the labour force, for attendance at school and for sex.

The second step makes use of the index by multiplying the increase in the index by labour's share of the national income. Thus if labour's share of the national income was 70% and the education index rose by 20% between two years, then the increase in national income due to education should have increased by $(.20 \times 0.70) = 14\%$ over this period. Thus if the annual rate of per capita growth in national income was 2% per annum, then the contribution of education would be 14% of 2% i.e. 0.28 percentage points of growth each year.

Denison has also attempted to explain the slower rate of economic growth experienced by the USA in the 1970s.[8] Factors which might be responsible include changes in personal characteristics of workers (e.g., effort exerted), changes in government or union restrictions on the efficient use of resources and in the legal and human environment (e.g., worker safety, pollution, crime). Whatever the precise cause, Denison's work suggests that the change in the contribution of the residual accounts for most of the changes in the growth rate. The residual is something of a rag bag of items and interaction among its components complicates the analysis. Thus in a review of Denison's work, Stone suggests that there has been a reduction in the work effort because people prefer to work for themselves or unofficially for others as part of the 'hidden economy'. This means they have less energy left for work in the regular economy, and this is tolerated by employers who are giant companies and bureaucracies. If this kind of argument is true then that part of the residual which is attributable to advances in knowledge would have to be revised upwards and the other components correspondingly revised downwards.[9]

Most of Denison's work has been concerned with the USA, but he has analysed other countries and other writers have used his methods to look at growth in their own countries. The results show wide variations as shown in Table 4.1.

There are several possible explanations of these variables. The figures are for a period not long after the Second World War when there was substantial physical rebuilding in Western Europe and this might have reduced the relative contribution of education so that more recent

Table 4.1 *The Contribution of Education to Economic Growth 1950–1962*

Country	*Rate of Growth in National Income*	*Contribution of Education as %*
USA	3.3	15
UK	2.3	13
Belgium	3.2	13
France	4.9	6
Germany	7.2	2
Italy	6.0	7
Argentina	3.2	16
Brazil	5.5	3
Mexico	6.0	1

Source: The figures for the USA and Europe are from Denison, E. F., *Why Growth Rates Differ*, Brookings Institute, 1967, and those for Latin America from Correa, H., 'Sources of Economic Growth in Latin America', *Southern Economic Journal*, No. 37, July 1970, pp. 17–31.

estimates may give a larger figure. Psacharopoulos analyses a larger sample of countries and after dividing them into three groups concludes that the contribution of education to growth is generally higher in the less developed countries.[10]

An alternative explanation for these figures arises from the limitations of the data and the methodology. As Machlup points out: 'One should realise that nothing in modern economics is more speculative than quantative empirical research. No one ought to be surprised, therefore if the results obtained by different investigators differ widely'.[11] One reason for this is that the data is always inaccurate, particularly in less developed countries, where statistical services are inadequate, and where much production is for self sufficiency and so is impossible to measure at all accurately. Then, the researcher has to make various assumptions; Denison for example assumes that the quality of education does not change and that it is easy to substitute one type of labour for another. In the last chapter we discussed the relationship between education and income and that issue affects the results here, because allowing for differential ability will have a significant effect on the results, reducing the contribution of education by up to 10%.[12] Moreover differences in method, such as the treatment of on the job training will have an effect on the results. An example of the uncertainty is given by Moreh. Using what he terms as the 'earnings' method, which allows for training and making no allowance for differential ability, he calculates the contribution of education to economic growth to be over 28%; using an alternative method which omits training but allows for differential ability the contribution can be as low as 9%.

The conclusion of this section must be that it is extremely difficult to calculate the contribution of education to economic growth; that the effect varies considerably between countries but is often substantial, and that all estimates must be treated with a great deal of caution. As Bowman points out, it is quite irresponsible to generalise, and serious researchers such as Schultz and Denison do not attempt to do so.

> Nevertheless, their findings are being misapplied around the world – and sometimes by men of high levels of supposed expertise, certified under the wing of international agencies, as well as in the utterances of small politicos. The fact that what education can do depends on other, complementary developments . . . is conveniently but unjustifiably ignored.[13]

Cost-Benefit Analysis

Another way of assessing the economic effects of education is to make use of cost-benefit analysis. Though this does not show clearly how education contributes to growth, it is a potentially useful technique for assessing the contribution an investment in education might make to the economy. The essence of the technique is that it treats educational expenditure just as a businessman might treat some item of spending in a factory. If the businessman is considering some new project, he will assess the costs and benefits and decide if the project is worthwhile.

Prest and Turvey have defined cost-benefit analysis as:

> a practical way of assessing the desirability of projects, where it is important to take a long view (in the sense of looking at repercussions in the further, as well as the nearer, future) and a wide view (in the sense of allowing for side effects of many kinds on many persons, industries, regions, etc.) i.e. it implies the enumeration and evaluation of all the relevant costs and benefits.[14]

Before we can discuss appropriate techniques for evaluation it is necessary to understand what is meant by *discounting*. This procedure is necessary because the returns and costs of an investment are often spread over many years and this creates problems. Even with the effects of inflation removed, people would prefer £100 now to £100 in a year's time. There are three main reasons for this. The first is uncertainty: during the year either or both parties to the transaction might die, or disappear or go bankrupt. Secondly, receiving money now means the individual could invest it and obtain interest. Finally receiving the money now rather than in a year means the individual can choose when to spend it. Thus when there is considerable uncertainty and interest rates are high people would much prefer the money now. If a ninety year old offers to pay in a year, the wise man asks for the money rather earlier! The technical expression for this situation is to say that future returns (and costs) should be discounted, the amount of the discount depending on the factors just mentioned. Thus if the income is fairly certain (as with a pension or from the government) and interest rates are low, the discount may be only 10%; that is to say an individual may be indifferent between £90 now and £100 in a year. In other cases the discount may be much greater so that the individual equates (say) £70 now with £100 in a year.

The choice of discount rate is a complex matter and the subject of a good deal of argument in the literature.[15] Some writers believe that the correct rate for a public sector investment is the rate of interest the government has to pay when it borrows money, whilst others believe that this is too low a rate because lending to the government is 'safe' and the public sector ought to compete by calculating its discount rate at the higher private sector rate.

The two main techniques of cost-benefit analysis are called the *net present value* and the *internal rate of return*.

The net present value rule says that projects should be selected where the present value of benefits exceeds the present value of costs. By 'present value' is meant the future earnings and costs discounted at an appropriate rate. Table 4.2 may clarify the technique. It shows an appraisal of the technique using the net present value rule in a hypothetical situation where an investment of £500 is made in year 0. The returns start one year later and amount to £100 a year for 10 years. These are discounted at 10% so that an actual receipt of £100 in year one is worth £90; a receipt of £100 two years hence has to be discounted twice and is therefore only worth £81. As the costs arise during the current year in this case they do not need to be discounted.

Table 4.2 *Net Present Value at Discount Rate of 10%*

Year	*Actual Cost*	*Net Present Value of Costs*	*Actual Benefits*	*Net Present Value of Benefits*
0	500	500	0	0
1			100	90
2			100	81
3			100	72.9
4			100	65.6
5			100	59.1
6			100	53.1
7			100	47.8
8			100	43.0
9			100	38.7
10			100	34.9
Total	500	500	1000	586.1

In this case the net present value of costs is £500 and the net present value of the benefits is £586 and the net present value would therefore indicate that the project should go ahead. However if the discount rate were higher this might not be the case. For example, if the chosen discount rate was 15% the annual figures for the net present value of the benefits would be £82, £72, £61, £52 and after ten years would be less than £20 a year giving a total net present value of £455; in other words the net present value of the costs would be greater than that of the benefits and the project would not be worthwhile.

The second technique in cost-benefit analysis is called the internal rate of return. The method here is to calculate that rate of discount which will make the present value of the costs equal to the present value of the benefits. The rate of discount is called the internal rate of return and the project should go ahead when the internal rate of return exceeds the chosen discount rate. In the example given earlier the benefits were greater than the costs at a discount rate of 10% but lower than the costs at a discount rate of 15%. Thus at some discount rate between 10% and 15% the discounted benefits will equal the discounted costs. The actual discount rate which will equate the costs and benefits is just under 13% and this is the internal rate of return.

Cohn gives another example which may clarify the procedures. Imagine a project which includes an outlay of £1000 in time period 0 and benefits of £100 a year for 20 years at a discount rate of 5%. The net present value of benefits would add up to £1246; the costs would be £1000 and the net present value rule would suggest that the project go ahead. Alternatively the internal rate of return could be calculated by a series of approximations and is in fact 7.75%. Since the chosen discount rate is 5% the project should go ahead.[16]

The two techniques give the same advice in almost all cases, though problems may arise when the stream of benefits fluctuates from positive returns to negative and back to positive, or when it is desired to put possible projects in order of priority, for then the criteria may lead to different conclusions. In practice the internal rate of return is most often quoted, if only because it is more meaningful to most people to talk about a return of 13% rather than a net present value of £86.

When cost-benefit analysis is applied to education, the usual procedure is:

1 decide on what is being measured – for example the return on a first degree;
2 obtain data on costs such as that presented at the end of Chapter 2;
3 obtain data on the output of education for the particular course as discussed in Chapter 3;
4 analyse the costs and benefits as outlined here (but almost certainly using a computer) to obtain the net present value and/or the internal rate of return.

Such a brief summary may make the procedure seem simple; but in practice it is difficult and subject to considerable limitations so that the results must be treated with a good deal of caution.

The first reason for this is that the data on which the calculation is based are subject to many errors. So far as the costs are concerned, some of the data may be accurate – for example expenditure on teachers' salaries, but a subjective element enters the calculation when these figures are adjusted to allow for factors such as the time university teachers spend teaching on other courses and on research. Much less accurate is data for earnings foregone where huge uncertainties may exist. However these pale into insignificance when the attempt is made to quantify benefits. It is simply not possible to quantify most of the externalities resulting from education, indeed it is difficult to say if most of them are large or small. Consequently almost all the cost-benefit analyses of education ignore all the benefits except the extra income resulting from the course. They therefore underestimate the returns to education; the extent of this underestimate depends on the size of the excluded benefits. The observant reader may notice that such a procedure fails to observe the basic principle of cost-benefit analysis which was developed at the beginning of this section – that is to 'enumerate and evaluate *all* the relevant costs and benefits'.

There are other, more technical, objections and difficulties. Thus the choice of an appropriate discount rate is a crucial aspect of any cost-benefit decision, particularly when benefits will be received over a long period, for a high discount rate will soon greatly reduce the net present value. As most educational investments create long lasting benefits, this is of crucial importance. Other problems have already been discussed in the last chapter. Do higher earnings represent greater productivity? What allowances should be made for intelligence and family background? When all these problems are considered it is clear that the results of cost-benefit analyses in education must be considered with caution.

There have, however, been many studies in this area, particularly in the USA. Cohn summarises many of these and shows that the returns to society on investment in elementary schooling seem to vary between 11.6% and 17.8%.[17] Social rates of return to secondary schooling are a little lower, most results being between 10% and 14%. Most of the studies have been on returns to college education, and here again results vary, in part because of differing samples of students and of differing estimates of costs and benefits and of adjustments for ability. The returns vary between just over 10% to just over 14%, though there is some evidence that the rate of return seems to be lower in recent years.

Returns to postgraduate education tend to be much lower, largely because the earnings foregone part of costs are very large. There are wide variations in returns, depending in part on the course. Some studies have found negative returns (i.e., the costs are greater than the benefits) whilst others obtain returns in single figures. These kinds of results have led to some suggestions that there is over investment in postgraduate education.

There are many American studies of particular areas. Returns to vocational education vary considerably – one study of vocational education in high school gave a return of 56%, but others show very low returns. The internal rate of return on education is usually lower for blacks than whites, perhaps because blacks receive poorer quality education or because they tend to receive lower incomes as a result of discrimination. The position is less clear when returns for men and women are compared, some studies showing higher returns for men and some for women.

There have been rather fewer studies in Britain, partly because there is a shortage of available raw data on the relationship between education and earnings. The first significant study was by Henderson-Stewart who used data obtained from a random sample of 6500 males in the early 1960s. The data was very crude – for instance 'income' included unearned incomes rather than earnings and there were some non-responders. His results suggested that the social rate of return for three years of education beyond the age of fifteen was 12.5%. The return to higher education was around 6.5%.[18]

Another study was completed by Morris and Ziderman using data obtained in 1968 by following up the educationally qualified revealed in the 1966 Sample Census. The results are given in Table 4.3.

The table shows that returns to society vary considerably. The lowest returns are to those with a first degree continuing to take a masters degree where the return is less than 0%. At the other extreme the return to educating a male with ONC so that he obtains HNC is over 20%. These figures make no allowance for externalities, and much of the difference in the returns is due to variations in earnings foregone. HNC is a part-time course so the opportunity cost is largely student's leisure time which was not quantified. On the other hand, the figure for earnings foregone was very large for a graduate proceeding to post-graduate studies.

The pattern of results shown here was also found in a study of sixty eight factories in the electrical engineering industry by Layard *et al.*[19] Considering only the benefits measured by pay, the social rate of return to undergraduate education in science and engineering was about 8% per annum. The return to doctoral training was about 4% and for a master's degree the social return was negative. The highest returns were 14% to HNC.

There have been many studies of returns to education in other countries. Psacharopoulos collated these and his calculations suggest that the average return to primary education is 25%, just over 13% for secondary, and over 11% for higher education.[20] However these averages conceal very large variations between countries.

Table 4.3 *Rates of Return to Society from Investment in Education 1966–67 %*

Males	*A*	*B*
A level/non-qualified	7.7	6.9
ONC/non-qualified	7.9	7.0
HNC/ONC	>20	>20
First Degree/A level	12.1	9.2
Masters/first degree	2.6	<0
Females		
First Degree/non-qualified	7.9	5.8
First Degree/A level	6.5	3.8

Source: Morris, V., Ziderman, A., 'The Economic Return on Investment in higher education in England and Wales', *Economic Trends*, No. 211, May 1971, pp. xx–xxxi, Table E.

Notes 1 Column A gives the return after removing research costs from the direct costs and making no adjustments for ability. Column B gives a lower return because it inflates costs by making no allowance for research and it reduces returns by allowing for ability by reducing annual earnings by one third.

2 The figure for females of First Degree/A level is an underestimate because the data for earnings of women with A level was too high.

From all these studies it is possible to draw out some conclusions. It seems that the rate of return falls as the level of schooling rises. This is probably because the earnings foregone on primary education are very small, but it does suggest that in developing countries more effort should be made to expand primary education, if necessary at the expense of higher education. This is a tentative suggestion, because there are other factors involved, for example there may be political pressure to expand higher education, or external funds may be available for this. Moreover, returns vary over time and a cost-benefit analysis only suggests directions; it does not say how much a programme should be expanded, for the expansion may itself change the returns. If educating electricians gives a high return on investment and then more electricians are trained, this may bring down their wages, so the return on investment will fall.

Psacharopoulos also compared returns by sex. As with the American data the results were varied. Of twenty one cases fourteen showed higher returns for men; the other seven had higher returns for women. The difference in favour of men was greatest at primary level.

So far this chapter has concentrated on social rates of return; in other words the question being asked is – how would this benefit society? It is also possible to analyse private rates of return; that is to say, will it pay the individual to take a particular course? Different results are obtained here, because both costs and benefits vary from those to society. The private individual often does not pay direct costs, such as teachers' pay which comes from the state, and the net earnings foregone are reduced because many students receive grants. For these reasons private rates of return are almost always greater than social returns.

Ziderman used the census data mentioned earlier to calculate private rates of return in 1966–67. After reducing returns by a third to allow for ability he estimated that the returns to GCE A level were 8.5%; those with A level who went on to complete a first degree received 20%; and those with a first degree who completed a masters received 16.5%.[21] These figures were for males and omit some benefits; for example a major benefit of A level is the option to continue education. The results show very high rates of return, though there are huge variations in these figures for particular individuals and large variations for particular groups such as teachers. If these were excluded the returns would be higher.

There have been a number of studies of private rates of return to teachers. Hinchcliffe calculated rates of return to male teachers taking an Open University degree. The returns depended in part on the age of the teacher and substantially on the value placed on leisure time foregone. If this was valued at zero the return for a thirty-year-old teacher was 39%; if leisure time was valued at 75 pence (in 1971) the return was reduced to 8%.[22] Birch and Calvert also calculate private rates of return for teachers. They increased teachers actual income by a month's pay to allow for long holidays. Their results were; male graduates 14%; male non-graduates just under 10%, female graduates 30%, female non-graduates 30%.[23] These very high returns for women teachers are in part a measure of the low pay available to women in other occupations and would be expected to fall when and if women have equal career prospects in all occupations. Atkinson's work also suggests very high rates of return for teachers staying on at college to obtain a B Ed degree compared to those obtaining just a Teacher's Certificate, though there were considerable variations, from 25% for men teachers in primary schools to 38% in secondary schools. Women's returns were 33% in primary and 36% in secondary.[24] These high rates may be reduced as teaching moves to an all graduate profession.

Private returns have been analysed for other occupations. Wilson calculated the private rates of return to becoming a professional scientist or engineer. In 1967/68 these were all between 14% and 15.5%; by 1976/77 the rates had fallen to between 8% and 10% depending on the particular science. He suggests various reasons for the decline. The level of student grants had fallen in real terms and incomes policies may have had a greater impact on higher incomes. Unqualified people had relatively large increases (which raised the earnings foregone costs). However he concludes that the major factor has been the very large increase in the number of scientists and engineers and that this increase has brought down the relative wage of the group.[25]

Psacharopoulos's survey of other countries mentioned earlier shows considerable variation in private rates of return between countries, but confirms the generalisation that these are almost always higher than social returns, and that the difference is bigger in the case of higher education because governments give this sector bigger subsidies. In developing countries both social and private returns to education were greater than those in developed countries. This difference was particularly large for private returns which were especially large in the poorer countries, suggesting that these offer relatively large subsidies to education which reduce the private costs. Another characteristic of private returns is that these are much higher for the final year of a course than for earlier years.

Private rates of return have been used to study the demand for education. Thus if the returns are high for studying medicine and low for agriculture, one would expect medical schools to be full and agricultural colleges finding it difficult to fill their places. Similarly, if children think that there are high returns to staying on at school or to higher education, it seems reasonable to assume that many of them will choose to extend their education. If they believe that returns to staying on are poor, they may choose to leave.

There is some evidence that children's *expected* private rates of return are fairly close to actual returns. Using a sample of just under 3000 children in English schools, Williams and Gordon asked them to estimate future earnings and then calculated that sixteen-year old boys perceived the private rate of return to staying on to age eighteen as 17%, with a further 10% for continuing to take a degree. For girls the figures were lower, 9% for staying on at school and 8% for higher education.[26] They compared these anticipated results with actual results obtained by Psacharopoulos and Layard who used a sample of 7000 employed males to calculate private returns of 12% for GCE A level and 10% for a first degree.[27] These returns are all for incomes after tax has been deducted. The research does not demonstrate that young people *are* influenced by perceived rates of return when making educational decisions, but they do suggest that pupils are aware of rates of return, which is an essential first step.

Any conclusion to this section must be tentative given the limitations of the studies. However it does seem that in many countries the return society gets on its investment in education is comparable to its investments in other areas of the economy. In developing countries in particular, there seems to be a tendency to invest too little in primary education compared to higher education, whilst in the UK we under invest in part-time education. In both cases the reason may be the relatively high prestige of full-time higher education courses, and there are strong social and political pressures to expand full-time higher education.

The difference between private and social rates of return may have serious repercussions, particularly in poorer countries. The demand for education is determined by individuals who anticipate high financial returns on their studies. Even though individuals do not calculate rates of return, they are aware that educated people earn much more than the less educated, that employers often give preference to those with qualifications and that much of the cost of education is borne by the state. On the other hand the supply of educational places is largely the function of government which is under considerable pressures to expand the system. If it does so it may exacerbate the problem of unemployment among the educated. This kind of analysis has led to suggestions that governments should give greater weight to prospective employment opportunities when planning educational expansion.[28]

Manpower Planning

This link between education and jobs is of crucial importance to those who approach economic growth via an interest in manpower planning. In the 1960s a number of writers analysed the relationship between levels of education and national income. Bowman and Anderson analysed literacy rates in eighty three countries. Their research suggested that if exceptional countries such as those with oil were excluded, adult literacy rates over 40% were needed for per capita incomes to be higher than $300 and that 90% literacy seemed to be needed for incomes to pass $500 per head.[29] However, though literacy may be a necessary condition for development, it is not a sufficient condition, for it is possible to have relatively high levels of literacy in a country but for it to have a low income per head. Moreover the correlation between literacy and income may exist, not because literacy causes incomes to rise, but because a country with high incomes can make available sufficient resources to reduce illiteracy. Bowman and Anderson found evidence to support the latter proposition when they examined incomes and enrolments in school in the 1930s and 1950s. Their results showed that income levels in the 1930s could be used to predict enrolments in the 1950s, but the level of enrolments in the 1930s showed only a low correlation with incomes twenty years later. In other words, the research suggested that the causal link was from income to education rather than vice versa. In any case 'literacy' is such a broad concept and can be measured in so many ways that comparisons of levels of literacy between countries are highly speculative. Developing countries have put considerable resources into literacy campaigns, often of the type 'each one teach one', where each educated person is expected to teach someone to read. In the past two or three decades, there have been so many adult literacy projects around the world that it would not be unduly cynical to suggest that everyone has learned to read twice! These campaigns often show few long term results, for those who achieve minimal standards often subsequently revert to illiteracy. It is not hard to suggest reasons why a literate population will be more likely to develop economically than an illiterate one, but this is of little use from a perspective of resource allocation. What is required is a decision on what resources to devote to literacy and what resources to devote to other uses which may prove to be more productive. Whilst there are strong social, educational and economic arguments in favour of extending literacy, this may or may not be the best way to promote growth. In any case the relationship between literacy and development may change over time, probably in the direction of requiring more literacy, if only because developing countries must interact and compete with countries having rising educational standards.

Literacy is only one aspect of the complex relationship between education and economic growth. Thus Razin looked at data for eleven countries in the 1950s and 1960s and found a positive correlation between the percentage of population aged 15–19 enrolled in secondary education and per capita national income. His results suggest that an increase in the percentage enrolled in secondary education would lead to an increase in the rate of growth of national income.[30]

However, evidence from the past is not necessarily applicable to the future and experience in one country cannot easily be applied in another. That there is a relationship between education and growth would be generally accepted; that there is a universal and generally applicable relationship that can be used to aid development is less certain. It is thus open to governments to adopt differing strategies for education. One possible approach is for the government to adopt a minimalist approach towards manpower; in other words, to leave it to market forces. The argument runs as follows: if there is a shortage of some skills in an economy – say of engineers – employers will have to raise wages to attract staff and to keep their existing staff. They may also recruit engineers from abroad. These high wages will encourage students to take engineering subjects and thus relieve the shortage. If this kind of argument is accepted there is little need for governments to plan manpower, for the rationale for planning arises from the limitations of a laissez-faire approach.

One limitation is that the process described above takes a long period of time to operate. The shortage takes time to make itself apparent to employers, then there is a lag whilst they decide whether or not to raise wages for this group. When this is done it may take years for the higher rewards for engineers to become widely known, and finally the training itself takes several years – assuming that there are places available. If there are insufficient places available, it will take a considerable amount of time before these can be expanded. Moreover, if the high earnings are well known, very large numbers might seek to enter the professions so that the ultimate result is over-production and possible unemployment. Thus the central argument in favour of planning manpower is that it takes many years for market forces to produce skilled manpower, that eventually too many will train for particular occupations, and that this is costly to the country.

The argument for planning also rests on the assumption that shortage of highly skilled manpower constitutes a bottleneck to economic growth. In other words more highly trained people are required if output is to expand. It is also assumed that it is possible to specify the number and type of skills required for an expansion to take place. If a country decides to plan its economy, then the manpower aspects will also need to be planned.

There are a number of benefits said to derive from planning. Without planning, policies may be inconsistent. It is no use building a steel mill if there are not people with appropriate skills to run it. Moreover, whilst rate of return analysis may suggest which sectors of the education system should be expanded, the technique gives no indication of the precise number of places that should be provided. Forecasts of manpower needs do provide actual figures of targets. Drawing up a plan might help to clarify objectives and priorities; for the process of planning requires that objectives are specified, and this helps to make clear what must be achieved, what might be, and which objectives cannot be achieved.

There are many approaches to manpower planning, some of them extremely complex. Perhaps the simplest is just to ask employers what kind of workers they currently employ and how many they would expect to employ, in say five years time. The figures obtained in this survey can then be adjusted to take account of deaths and wastage and specific figures obtained for requirements in various occupations. This may sound to be a sensible approach, but it has serious limitations. Five years is not a long enough period to create educational facilities and train highly skilled manpower, but it is longer than most employers can forecast. There is a temptation for employers to suggest more than they will probably need, for an increase in the supply of skilled workers will be useful if expansion takes place, and if it does not, the suggestion costs employers nothing. Moreover, the requirements of employers will depend on factors such as future changes in national output and wages which are unknown. Thus it is not surprising that the results of such surveys are highly inaccurate. They have been used in the UK and are the source of many of the statements which suggest that there is a shortage of scientific and engineering manpower. Sir Solly Zuckerman, the chairman of the Committee on Scientific Manpower, reported to the

Robbins Committee 'we have discovered in our successive inquiries that one of the least reliable ways of finding out what industry wants is to go and ask industry'.[31]

Another approach to planning is to make international comparisons. The essence of this technique is to assume that countries go through stages as they develop, so that a poor country can use rather more developed ones as examples and take the amount of high level manpower used in those countries as targets. This technique has been used in a number of countries, but it has considerable limitations. There are many paths to development and what is appropriate for one country may not be so for another. Moreover, the procedure assumes that more educated countries have an efficient allocation of resources in the area of manpower, and this might not be so. Finally international comparisons into the relationship between educational and economic performance indicators show that these vary very widely from one country to another. Therefore it is very difficult for the administration to choose which country should be imitated.[32]

A rather more sophisticated approach is suggested by Parnes.[33] The various steps are:

1 Prepare an inventory of manpower for the current year, classifying the labour force by occupation, industry, education and age.
2 Estimate the total size of the available labour force for the target year.
3 Estimate total employment in each branch of the economy for the target year.
4 For each of these branches allocate the total employment to various occupations.
5 Specify the education required for these various occupations.
6 Estimate the supply of people with various educational qualifications based on present stocks, deaths and retirements.
7 Calculate the additional enrolments needed to meet the requirements.

This outline of the various steps skips over the difficulties. Clearly it is extremely difficult to 'estimate total employment in each branch of the economy', especially if the target year is several years in the future. One way to do this is to set some figure for Gross National Product in the target year and to break this down by major sectors such as agriculture, manufacturing, or transport and to estimate the productivity of labour in each of these. This makes it possible to suggest that an increase in the output of, say, the coal industry of ten million tons would require so many additional workers with varying educational qualifications.

There are various criticisms made of the manpower requirements approach. Firstly, it is quite difficult to define what is an 'occupation', for there are several ways to do this. If occupation is defined by reference to the level of education and training required, then questions about the efficient utilisation of manpower are difficult to ask. If physicists are defined in terms of possession of a degree in physics, then it would be difficult to discover if physicists are working as salesmen or as school counsellors. An alternative is to define occupation by reference to the nature of the job, and this is extremely difficult.

Moreover, the manpower planning approach usually involves step five mentioned previously; that is to specify the education required for certain occupations. Sometimes this is done by specifying the numbers of years of education required. Even within a particular country people in the same occupation may have very different levels of education; across countries the variations are enormous. Thus the EEC has been trying for several years to work towards comparability of qualifications, but has found the task very difficult. There is clearly room for much discussion in determining how much education is required for a particular occupation. Moreover some approaches to manpower planning ignore the possibility of substituting one kind of manpower for another. It may be more efficient for poor countries to employ five medical assistants rather than one doctor. The careful reader may have noticed that the steps outlined previously say nothing about efficiency, or even about costs. Clearly such considerations can be added, but they are not a central point of the process. If the planning process suggests that fifty veterinary surgeons are required, the tendency is to produce them rather than to see if more efficient ways of doing the work can be discovered.

Given the many and complex steps in the process it is not surprising that inaccuracies arise. The World Bank's Education Sector Policy Paper points out that 'the problem of formation of skills within the formal system lies in part in the difficulty of forecasting accurately the requirements for specific skills in the economy' and goes on to suggest that forecasts of needed manpower made in the 1960s have not usually remained valid.[34] The situation has not changed much since Blaug wrote in 1970: 'All the existing evidence shows that we do not yet know how to forecast beyond three or four years with anything remotely resembling the margins of error that are regarded as tolerable in general economic forecasting'.[35] Predictions for high level manpower requirements a decade or more in the future are indeed 'social science fiction'.

Yet this does not necessarily invalidate the practice. Manpower planners do not claim to forecast what *will* happen; rather they seek to determine what manpower resources will probably be required *if* a particular plan is to be fulfilled. Thus if the target for national income is not met because of other factors, such as an increase in the price of oil, the manpower target may also not be achieved.

Since governments are not content to leave the future supply of skilled manpower entirely to market forces, various ways have been suggested for them to intervene.

In Britain, dissatisfaction at current methods of manpower forecasting, an essential part of any intervention, were made apparent by submissions to a House of Commons Committee.[36] The Institute of Manpower Studies commented bluntly 'past attempts at manpower forecasting have been largely unsuccessful', and went on to suggest reforms such as better information about current manpower needs and the establishment of a forum with sufficient resources to monitor the employment of qualified manpower and to assess future manpower needs on a regular basis.

An alternative approach was suggested by Williams and Fulton in a separate memorandum to the same committee. They suggested that there should be a more serious investment in counselling and guidance so that potential students should receive information not only on entry qualifications and curriculum, but also on employment prospects several years hence. This should be reinforced by a greater provision of systematic part-time and recurrent education. These suggestions would help individuals respond to market changes more effectively. In a separate paper these authors point out that any country which wishes to use manpower forecasts as the main basis for planning higher education needs to devote considerable resources to this activity and that many of the difficulties connected with manpower planning could be alleviated by a greater commitment to lifelong education.[37]

What Kind of Education?

So far this chapter has tended to discuss 'education' in a very general sense; but in reality choices have to be made *within* education. Machlup suggests that there may be a conflict of objectives in determining educational priorities in developing countries.[38] Social justice considerations would suggest that ensuring all children go to primary school was an important objective. However, this may conflict with the objective of efficiency, for drop-out rates are very high in many countries, and children who leave school after only two or three years will have attained very few long-lasting accomplishments.

What is required for economic development is the right quantities of particular kinds of education and neither cost-benefit analysis nor manpower techniques can indicate unequivocally what these are, though both techniques can give useful indications. Whilst what is appropriate for one country may not be for another, it may be that the poorest countries should aim at, say, half of their children completing primary school with few drop-outs, that the most talented of these should go on to secondary education to provide the secretaries, nurses, supervisors and technicians and other middle level manpower required. Relatively few should continue into higher education.

It is not enough to decide the levels of education, for the kind of education is also important. There is often a temptation to argue that because an economy needs particular skills it would be efficient to provide vocational schools. Philip Foster pointed out the fallacy in this some years ago.[39] He argued that vocational education provided in formal educational institutions could not become an effective method of accelerating economic development. This was because general education was a necessary foundation for vocational education which should be closely linked with on the job training. The World Bank has recognised this, pointing out that: 'General education has been found in many countries to increase the productivity of workers, making them more self-reliant, more adaptive to new situations, and, above all, more trainable.'[40]

In pointing out the 'vocational school fallacy', Foster was writing in the context of Africa, but a similar fallacy may exist in the richer countries of the world. When economic development slows down, it is easy for politicians and others to call for educational reform and to suggest that education should become more relevant to the economy. Thus the DES document on *The School Curriculum* claimed that 'the 5–16 curriculum cannot, and should not, remain static, but must respond to the changing demands made by the world outside school.'[41] The implication of this is that particular emphasis should be given to maths and science and especially to the use of computers. This is a rather simplistic view of development. It seems to equate growth with industrialisation, industrialisation with engineering, and the latter with studying science at school. All of these links are grossly over simplified. There is very little evidence to support the hypothesis that if students study subjects such as physics, economic growth will be faster than if they studied economics or geography. The link between school subjects and economic development is complex and uncertain, and it may be that the attitudes engendered by schools are more important than the specific subjects studied.

References

1 Harbison, F. H., *Human Resources as the Wealth of Nations*, Oxford, 1973, Ch. 1.
2 Mishan, E. J., *The Costs of Economic Growth*, Penguin, 1969, p. 2.
3 Hicks, N. L., 'Growth v. Basic Needs: Is There a Trade off?', *World Development*, Vol. 7, 1979, pp. 985–94.
4 Lewis, W. A., *The Theory of Economic Growth*, George Allen & Unwin, 1955.
5 Haddad, W. D., 'The World Bank' – Education Sector Policy Paper: a summary', *Comparative Education*, Vol. 17 No. 2, June 1981, pp. 127–39.
6 Schultz, T. W., 'Education and Economic Growth' in Henry, N. B., ed.,

Social Forces Influencing American Education, University of Chicago Press, 1961.

7 Denison, E. F., *Accounting for United States Economic Growth 1929–1969*, Brookings Institution, 1974.

8 Denison, E. F., *Accounting for Slower Economic Growth: The United States in the 1970s*, Brookings Institute, 1979.

9 Stone, R., 'Whittling away at the Residual – some thoughts on Denison's Growth Accounting', *Journal of Economic Literature*, Vol. XVIII, December 1980, pp. 1539–43.

10 Pscharapoulos, G., *Returns to Education: An International Comparison*, Elsevier, 1973, Ch. 7.

11 Machlup, F., *Education and Economic Growth*, University of Nabraska Press, 1970, p. 10.

12 Moreh, J., 'Human Capital and Economic Growth: United Kingdom 1951–61', *Economic and Social Review*, September 1971, pp. 73–93.

13 Bowman, M. J., 'Perspectives on Education and Development', in Wykstra, R. A., *Human Capital Formation and Manpower Development*, Free Press, 1971.

14 Prest, A. R. and Turvey, R., 'Cost Benefit Analysis: a Survey', *Economic Journal*, Vol 75, December 1965, pp. 683–735.

15 See Feldstein, M. S., 'The Social Time Preference Discount Rate', *Economic Journal*, Vol. LXXIV, June 1964, pp. 360–79, Baumol, W. J., 'On the Social Rate of Discount', *American Economic Review*, Vol. LVIII, December 1968, pp. 788–802.

16 Cohn, E., *The Economics of Education*, 2nd ed., 1979, Ballinger, p. 98.

17 *ibid*. p. 113f.

18 Henderson-Stewart, D., 'Appendix: Estimates of the Rate of Return to Education in Great Britain', *Manchester School*, Vol. 33 No. 3, 1965, pp. 252–61.

19 Layard, P. R. G., Sargan, J. D., Ager, M. E. and Jones, D. J., *Qualified Manpower and Economic Performance*, Allen Lane, 1971, pp. 20–21.

20 Psacharapoulos, G., *op. cit.*, p. 64f.

21 Ziderman, A., 'Does it pay to take a degree?', *Oxford Economic Press*, Vol. 25 No. 2, July 1973, pp. 262–74.

22 Hinchcliffe, K., 'Teachers, the Open University and the Rates of Return', *Higher Education Review*, Vol. 3 No. 3, Summer 1971, pp. 49–55.

23 Birch, D. W. and Calvert, J. R., 'How Profitable is Teaching?', *Higher Education Review*, Vol. 6 No. 1, Autumn 1972, pp. 35–44.

24 Atkinson, G. B. J., 'The Value of a B Ed degree', *Higher Education Review*, Vol. 7 No. 3, Summer 1975, pp. 60–63.

25 Wilson, R. A., 'The Rate of Return to becoming a Qualified Scientist or Engineer in Great Britain 1966–1976', *Scottish Journal of Political Economy*, Vol. 27 No. 1, February 1980, pp. 41–62.

26 Williams, G. and Gordon, A., 'Perceived Earnings Functions and Exante Rates of Return to Post Compulsory Education in England', *Higher Education*, Vol. 10, 1981, pp. 199–227.

27 Psacharopoulos, G. and Layard, R., 'Human Capital and Earnings: British Evidence and a Critique', *Review of Economic Studies*, Vol. XLVI, 1979, pp. 485–503.

28 Edwards, E. O. and Todaro, M. P., 'Education and Employment in

Developing Countires', in Ward, F. C., ed., *Education and Development Reconsidered*, Praeger, 1974.

29 Bowman, M. J. and Anderson, C. A., 'Concerning the role of education in development' in Bowman, M. J., *et al.*, eds., *Readings in the Economics of Education*, UNESCO, 1968.

30 Razin, A., 'Economic Growth and Education: New Evidence', *Economic Development and Cultural Change*, Vol. 25, January 1977, pp. 317–24.

31 Robbins Report, *op. cit.*, Vol. B p. 432.

32 Lee Kiong-Hock and Psacharapoulos, G., 'International Comparisons of Educational and Economic Indicators Revisited', *World Development*, Vol. 7, 1979, pp. 995–1004.

33 Parnes, H. S., 'Manpower Analysis in Educational Planning' in Blaug, M., *Economics of Education*, Penguin, 1968.

34 Haddad, W. D., 'The World Bank: Education Sector Policy Paper: a summary', *Comparative Education*, Vol. 17 No. 2, June 1981, pp. 127–39.

35 Blaug, M., *op. cit.*, p. 159.

36 Memoranda submitted to the Education Science and Arts Committee of the House of Commons, *5th Report on the Funding and Organisation of Courses in Higher Education*, Vol. 2, HC 78 7/2 787/1, 4 June 1980, p. 443f and 459f.

37 Fulton, D., Gordon, A. and Williams, G., 'Higher Education and Manpower Planning: A Comparison of Planned and Market Economies', *Education Policy Bulletin*, Vol. 8 No. 1, Spring 1980, pp. 83–113.

38 Machlup, F., *Education and Economic Growth*, University of Nebraska Press, 1970, p. 24.

39 Foster, P., 'The Vocational School Fallacy in Development Planning' in Blaug, M., ed., *Economics of Education I*, Penguin, 1968.

40 Haddad, W. D., *op. cit.*, p. 132.

41 DES, *The School Curriculum*, HMSO, 1981.

5

Planning Teacher Numbers: A Case Study

Planning Education

For most goods and services, there is no need for government planning. Market forces of demand and supply provide a reasonably efficient allocation of goods as diverse as trousers and trombones. Education is rather different. In the market economy signals such as a change in prices convey information to producers and consumers about the availability and need for particular goods. These signals are not usually clear in education and this may mean that the available manpower will not match the requirements in the field. If market forces are not in operation in this area then the service must be planned.

Less theoretically, there is little alternative to planning education unless the existing system is radically changed. In most countries education is provided mainly by public authorities and is one of the largest industries. All large scale producers must plan for their future and the education industry is no exception. Indeed, since the time lags in 'producing' qualified people are so long, some kind of planning is even more essential.

Planning education in Britain is difficult because decision-making is so diffused: not only is the Scottish system very different, but some educational decisions are made by Welsh and some by English local authorities. Thus the power of the centre is limited. Moreover, even at the DES, the system has been administered rather than planned and the number of officials concerned with planning remains small.

Planning in the DES has often been criticised. Thus a former Minister of State for Higher Education argued that it was 'too passive, too narrowly conceived, too secret and too little based on a comparative assessment of priorities.'[1] These views are not untypical, though as Williams points out, it is a debatable point whether widespread public discussion, such as that stimulated by the 1977 'Great Debate' on secondary school curricula or the 1978 document on 'Higher Education into the 1990s' effectively results in either more democratic or more efficient policy making or planning.[2] Moreover British educational planners are not noticeably better or worse than those in other countries. The apparent lack of success may be due in part to inefficiency, but there are real difficulties. Planners must be cautious because the rewards of success are frequently much less than the penalties for being wrong. It is often less embarrassing to do nothing than to make an incorrect decision. Another reason is that planning depends on priorities and these change, sometimes very quickly when governments change. These factors also apply at local level,[3] and because power is diffuse the ability to implement plans may be limited.

It is therefore not surprising that little use has been made of manpower planning in the Western world, though France and Sweden have made more serious efforts to incorporate manpower forecasting into their higher education planning. In the UK the areas which have received most attention from the planners are those dealing with the training of teachers and doctors.

Planning teacher numbers is a particularly important part of planning education. This is because the teaching profession is one of the most important categories of highly educated and qualified manpower. More educated people work in the education industry than in any other, and it is therefore both the producer and consumer of educated manpower. An increase in the demand for highly educated workers will necessitate an expansion of education and perhaps require more teachers to make the extension possible.

The responsibility for ensuring that there are sufficient teachers belongs to the Secretary of State for Education. The 1944 Education Act gave him the duty to 'make such arrangements as he considers expedient for securing that there shall be sufficient facilities for the training of teachers . . . and accordingly, he . . . may give any local education authority such directions as he thinks necessary requiring them to establish, maintain, or assist any training college or other institution or to provide or assist the provision of any other facilities specified in the direction.' In practice this power means that the Secretary of State has directly controlled numbers in individual teacher training institutions. Each year these receive a letter from the Secretary telling them how many students they will be allowed to admit. The Secretary's powers are limited in that he cannot ensure that sufficient students will apply to fill these places, and of course he has no control over the pass rate.

The detailed work of the DES in this area is undertaken by a special Teachers Branch which is responsible not only for the national planning of initial teacher training, but also for such things as in-service training The DES receives advice from an official body called the Advisory Committee on the Training and Supply of Teachers. This body does not issue public reports but its deliberations are sometimes reported in the press.

The teacher requirement depends on three main factors: the number of people to be taught, the relationship between the number of people to be taught and the number of teachers, and the number of new teachers needed to replace those leaving the profession.

The number of people to be educated of course depends on the birth rate. This varies considerably over the years as shown in Table 5.1.

In the period between the Second World War and 1960 the number of births reached a height of 881 000 in 1947 and fell to a low of 667 000 in 1955. Variations such as this and those shown in the table clearly have considerable impact on the school system and it would make planning considerably easier if accurate forecasts of the birth rate could be made. This is impossible because there are so many factors which affect the number of children being born; in a brief survey Carter *et al.* mention the number of young people of marriageable age, the average age of marriage, the desirable size of family, contraception, and the amount of paid work undertaken by women which may lead them to compress the period of child bearing into fewer years. Another factor is that, if women's real earnings rise, there will be a tendency to have fewer children because the opportunity cost of children will have risen.[4] Some of these factors can be predicted, particularly the number of young people of marriageable age. As a large number of children were born in 1964 it is not difficult to predict that around twenty years later many of

Table 5.1 *Number of Live Births in England and Wales*

(*thousands*)

Year	*Number*	*Year*	*Number*
1960	785	1972	725
1961	811	1973	676
1962	839	1974	640
1963	854	1975	603
1964	876	1976	584
1965	863	1977	570
1966	850	1978	596
1967	823	1979	638
1968	819	1980	656
1969	798	1981	634
1970	784	1982	624
1971	783		

Source: Office of Population Census and Statistics, *Birth Statistics England and Wales* HMSO, 1981, Table 1.1, *Population Trends*, 29, HMSO, 1982, Table 9, and OPCS, *Monitor*, 1983.

Figure 5.1 Primary and Secondary Pupil Numbers

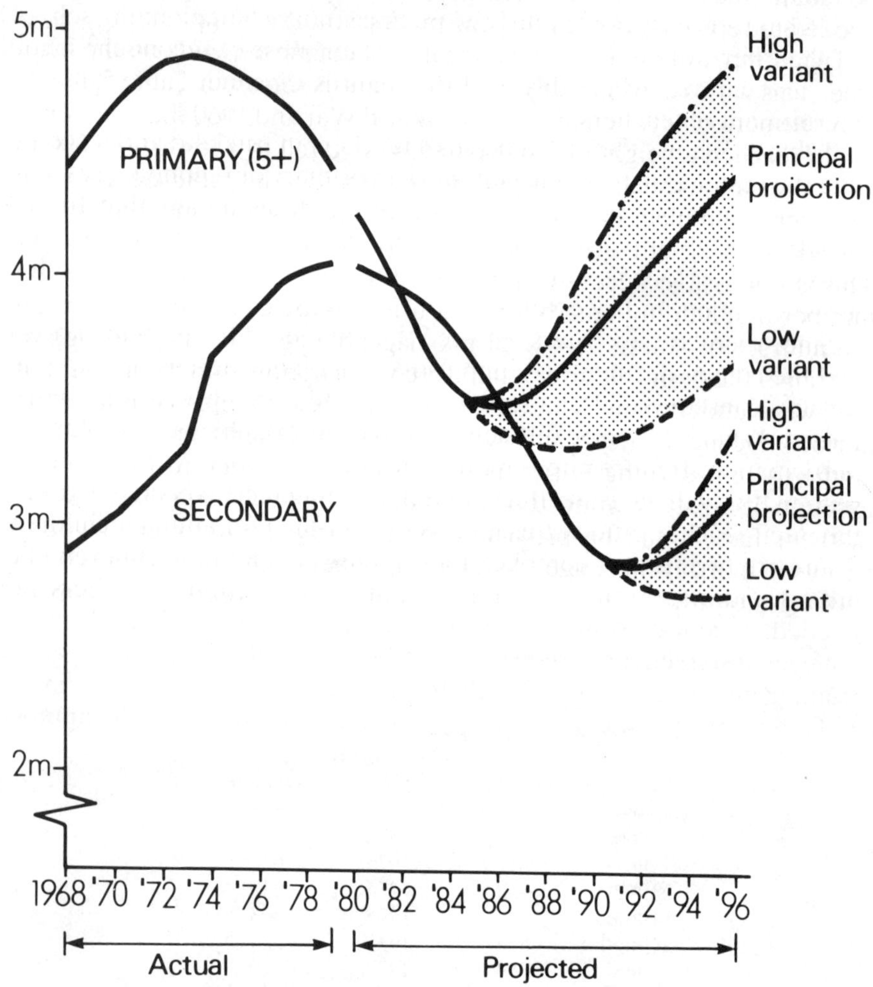

Source: DES, *Report on Education*, No. 96, November 1979.

them will marry and have children. What is less easy to determine are factors such as how many children they will want, and it is therefore not surprising that forecasts are inaccurate. Figure 5.1 shows the wide variation in pupil numbers which results from the adoption of differing assumptions about the fertility rate.

This uncertainty is obviously more important when planning schools and teachers for young children than it is for those of secondary school age and above, where actual birth figures give adequate time for recruitment of teachers.

Table 5.2 shows the distribution of teachers in England and it is clear that the vast majority of teachers work in primary or secondary schools. The small number of teachers in nursery schools means that from a planning viewpoint variations in the birthrate are not a major problem in this area, so long as some reception teachers are prepared to teach in nursery schools and vice-versa.

Since there are five years between the number of births being known and the commencement of compulsory schooling, there is time to plan for any consequential changes in teacher numbers which may be required. What is far more difficult to predict are the changes in voluntary participation. If more pupils wish to stay on at school beyond the age of sixteen, this will have an effect greater than might be expected, because the pupil-teacher ratio at this level is smaller than for younger children. There are two further complications. Firstly, some of the children may attend under-subscribed courses, so that no additional teachers are needed. Secondly, some of the children will move to further education colleges at sixteen, and some teachers there have not undergone teacher training but are recruited directly from industry.

Thus for the planner, the birth rate is a major influence on the number

Table 5.2 *Distribution of Teachers in England January 1981*

Nursery	1 600
Primary	178 800
Secondary	229 300
Misc/divided service	9 100
Further Education	93 900
Special Schools	18 000
Providing education other than at school	1 000
Total	531 700

Source: DES, *Statistical Bulletin* 14/81, September 1981.

Note: These figures include the full-time equivalent of part-time teachers and also teachers on secondment.

of teachers that will be required, but it is an influence that should give adequate time for variations to be made in the supply of teachers. Other influences may not.

Pupil-Teacher Ratios

However, the ratio of pupils to teachers is not fixed. An increase (or fall) in the number of pupils to be educated does not necessarily mean a proportionate change in the number of teachers that are required, because the ratio of pupils to teachers will also vary over time, as can be seen in Table 5.3.

Pupil-teacher ratios have been widely used in planning, forecasting and comparing educational systems. They seem easy to use and to understand. This apparent simplicity conceals a number of complications. The number of pupils will vary according to the time of the school year, and the teacher element can be calculated in different ways, for example by including or excluding relief teachers. So far as planning is concerned, the overall ratio will conceal wide variations in particular areas. In 1981 overall pupil-teacher ratios in England varied from 12.8 in the Isles of Scilly, and 14.2 in Inner London and in Brent, to over 20 in seven authorities, with a maximum of 20.7 in Somerset. These figures conceal wider variations with higher ratios in primary schools and in small schools.[5] The number of subjects taught and average teaching loads would also affect the calculations. If there is greater fragmentation of subjects and teachers have fewer class contact hours than previously, then more teachers will be needed.

Table 5.3 *Pupil-Teacher Ratios in England in 1971 and 1981*

	1971	*1981*
All schools	21.4	18.2
Maintained:		
Total	22.6	19.3
Nursery	19.1	19.7
Primary	27.0	22.6
Secondary	19.7	16.6
Non-maintained	13.7	12.5
Special	10.2	7.6

Source: DES, *Statistical Bulletin* 18/81, December 1981.

Note: The figures include full-time equivalent of part-time teachers.

An important influence is maximum class size. This is always larger than the pupil-teacher ratio because at any one time some teachers are not teaching. From a teaching point of view, class size seems more important than the pupil-teacher ratio, because what concerns teachers is the number of children they are expected to teach. There is a widespread belief that smaller classes will lead to higher attainment. They also lead to more employment for teachers, so it is not surprising that the teacher unions have persistently argued for them. In England there is no legal maximum class size, though under the *School Regulations* for most of the 1960s the maximum number of pupils on the class register of a primary school was supposed to be forty, whilst the figure for secondary schools was thirty. This regulation was revoked in 1969.[6]

The notion of a maximum size of class is not particularly useful in planning teacher numbers. The desirable maximum number of children in a group will depend on the activities of the children. Watching a film or listening to a lecture can be undertaken by large numbers of people with little diminution of learning. Moreover, the staffing needs of a particular institution will be greatly affected by the range of options it offers and the particular organisational arrangements it adopts. These factors will also affect the notion of *average* class size, which can be used as a tool to assess the teacher requirements of particular schools and, by a process of aggregation, for a county or country.[7] Clearly, if the average class size is fixed at, say, twenty five pupils, there will be some classes with over thirty children and perhaps some discontent among their teachers.

Whatever tool is used to estimate requirements, it will have to be acceptable by economic criteria. Even quite small changes in staffing standards cost large sums of money. In 1979 the pupil-teacher ratio in maintained secondary schools in England was 16.7.[8] To reduce this by just one would require nearly 15 000 teachers and about £150 million. Since tiny improvements are so expensive, it follows that they are vulnerable at times of economic stringency. This is one of the factors which makes planning teacher numbers so difficult. If national economic considerations make reductions in educational spending necessary, teacher numbers are almost certain to be cut, so that forecast requirements are not met. This is, in part, one reason why forecasts of teacher numbers go awry. If the economy is growing, more money is available for education and improvements can be made in pupil-teacher ratios, causing a 'shortage' of teachers. If the economy slows down – or declines – the reverse is true and teacher unemployment results.

The Supply of Teachers

The education industry has to compete with other industries and occupations to acquire its supply of labour. Therefore, in analysing the factors which affect the supply of labour, it is necessary to compare the net advantages of teaching compared with other occupations. These net advantages include not only the level of earnings but also other related factors, such as the stability of earnings and future prospects. In addition, non-monetary factors such as promotion prospects, conditions of work and fringe benefits must be considered.

The theory of net advantage suggests that competition between employers and workers will tend to equate net advantages between competing groups, so that changes in any of the factors will induce some workers to move. Thus if relative earnings fall in any occupation, some workers will leave that occupation. The theory also suggests that pay will tend to be lower in occupations with relatively pleasant working conditions.

It is clear that the earnings of teachers relative to other groups vary over time. Between 1948 and 1965 Vaizey and Sheehan calculate that the index of earnings for primary teachers rose from 100 to 296, that for secondary teachers rose to 288, whilst the index of average male earnings in industry rose to only 215.[9] One reason for the difference was the introduction of equal pay for women teachers. In the period 1965–1974 teachers' salaries deteriorated considerably in comparison with the average level of earnings in manufacturing industry.[10] The Houghton enquiry into teachers pay in 1974 increased teachers' salaries, but the unions felt that in subsequent years these fell behind competitive occupations, so that they called for another enquiry, and this was undertaken by the Standing Commission on Pay Comparability under Professor Clegg which led to an increase in teachers' pay. In their evidence to Clegg the management side suggested that there was no shortage of applicants for teaching, whilst the unions pointed out that the labour market for teachers was somewhat artificial, as the Government could control both supply (through the provision of teacher training) and demand (by allowing the pupil-teacher ratio to fluctuate).[11]

The Clegg Commission attempted to compare teaching with other occupations, but found this so difficult that they abandoned one approach. Apart from salaries, conditions of work and fringe benefits (such as sick pay, medical insurance, subsidized meals, discounts on purchases and cheap mortgages and loans) affect job comparisons, but perhaps the most important benefits are pensions, company cars, hours of work and holidays. The Commission believed that teachers held a relative advantage compared to other occupations so far as pensions were concerned and a disadvantage in relation to company cars. They also concluded 'that the teachers' advantage in relation to hours of work and holidays, if they have one, is less than is commonly supposed.'[12]

It is clear from all this that comparing occupations is difficult, and that the theory of net advantage cannot be proved – or disproved – with reference to teachers. However there is some evidence that salary levels affect recruitment. Zabalza *et al.* obtained access to the complete tapes of the teachers' record for 1963–72. They conclude that 'salaries do make a difference. The supply response to a change in wages is, as one might expect, larger for men graduates than for women. Not only starting salaries, but the whole salary profile, affect the numbers entering teaching.'[13] Men seem to be more sensitive to changes in career prospects, whilst women are more influenced by changes in immediate earnings.[14] In an earlier survey of British Research in Teacher Education, Lomax concluded that occupational choice was such a complex process that it was unlikely to be understood in terms of the data supplied by the blunt research instruments which were available. Thus few students had career plans or any knowledge of other jobs, so that a process of drift from school to college to school was an important explanation of teacher recruitment.[15]

So far the supply of teachers has been discussed largely in terms of entry to the profession. However this is inadequate, for two important influences on supply are wastage and re-entry.

Wastage causes particular problems for the planner. In 1973 the DES commented:

> Experience in the 1950s and 1960s showed how critically teacher supply planning is at the mercy of changes which may occur quickly in the rate at which teachers leave the profession. Future wastage rates, which may be powerfully influenced by demographic or economic factors, cannot be predicted with confidence but will have immediate effects.[16]

A simple back of an envelope calculation will show the importance of wastage. If there are approximately half a million teachers and the wastage rate is 10%, then each year some 50000 teachers will leave the profession; if the rate falls to 8%, then only 40000 will leave, and the authorities will need to recruit 10000 fewer teachers. This is the total output of many colleges and a fall in the wastage rate in the 1970s was a major reason why students leaving teacher training institutions could not obtain employment. Increases in the wastage rate have the opposite effect, and leave the authorities short of teachers with very little warning.

Several conclusions can be drawn from Table 5.4. Firstly, wastage rates fell substantially during the 1970s and, secondly, women are more likely to leave the profession than men. It is also clear that wastage rates are relatively low for those aged between thirty and sixty.

The overall wastage rate can be divided into sub-groups. The easiest of these to predict is wastage due to retirement, because DES records show the age structure of the teaching profession, so that it can calculate fairly well how many are likely to retire in any one year, though in recent years there has been a movement towards earlier retirement. Despite these uncertainties, the age structure of the profession is known and

Table 5.4 *Percentage Wastage Rates for Full-Time Teachers in Maintained Schools England and Wales*

Age	*1968/69* *Men*	*Women*	*1978/79* *Men*	*Women*
Under 25	11.5	16.3	6.4	8.4
25–29	9.4	23.1	5.9	16.6
30–34	6.4	14.9	3.6	13.9
35–39	4.5	8.1	2.5	6.0
40–44	3.4	5.5	2.3	3.7
44–49	2.6	4.2	1.8	3.2
50–54	2.0	3.7	2.4	3.7
55–59	2.8	5.1	4.7	7.0
60 and over	26.5	38.1	31.2	41.5
Overall	6.5	13.5	5.0	10.0

Source: DES, *Statistics of Education 1979*, Vol. 4, *Teachers*, HMSO, Table 11.

retirement can be predicted within relatively narrow limits. It is also easy to predict the number of teachers who will leave the profession due to ill health or death. This is because, whilst an individual school may have relatively large fluctuations in deaths or ill health, the number of teachers overall is so large that the 'law of large numbers' comes into operation. This suggests that, whilst it is not possible in social science to predict what any one individual (or even a few) will do, it is possible to make predictions for large groups. Thus public opinion polls can make predictions within specified limits of how people will vote and insurance companies can calculate the likelihood of accidents or death for particular groups.

In the past one very important group of leavers has been young women teachers. The statistics showed a very clear pattern. Women began teaching at twenty one or twenty two, got married and left the profession just before the birth of their first baby in their mid-twenties. Thus Zabalza *et al.* show that in 1972 over one in five of women teachers aged 25–29 left the profession.[17] This pattern was confirmed by other research. Ollerenshaw surveyed nearly four thousand women who had left teaching and concluded that the typical respondent 'first left full-time teaching for a substantial break in anticipation of the birth of a child after four or five years of full-time teaching.'[18] Since the early 1970s several changes have taken place. Women teachers have been affected by the factors which caused the general birth rate to fall, so that fewer teachers have left the profession for this reason. There are other factors which affect women teachers. Zabalza pointed out 'When unemployment increases and job opportunities for their husbands are scarce, decisions concerning marriage or child-birth can be postponed.'[19] This became more important as unemployment increased in the 1970s, and the wastage rate of young women was also reduced when legislation concerning maternity leave made it easier to return to teaching shortly after the birth of a baby. Thus in the 1970s fewer women teachers were likely to become pregnant; if they did give birth their withdrawal from teaching was likely to be short term. Changes such as these are difficult to predict.

For men teachers and for some women the pattern of wastage is different. Some people enter teaching, find they do not like it and leave. Others may enjoy it but decide the rewards are greater in other occupations and then leave. Their wastage rates are very high in the first few years after qualifying and then decline quite rapidly with age. If teachers' salaries and prospects seem to be relatively good, and if alternative jobs are difficult to find, then relatively few teachers will leave the profession. If teachers' pay seems poor and there are plenty of alternative jobs, then wastage rates will rise. In any event graduates with BAs or BScs will be more likely to leave than non-graduates or those with B Ed degrees, because their qualification is more widely acceptable. Given that relative wage rates and unemployment levels are difficult to forecast, it is not surprising that predictions of wastage rates several years in the future should be inaccurate.

The supply of teachers is not limited to those who have recently qualified. All those who have qualified and then left the profession are potential re-entrants and there may be more qualified ex-teachers than current practitioners. This forms a potential supply which may be important in case of shortage, though for those who have been some years away from school some re-training may be necessary. During the 1970s just over 10000 teachers a year re-entered maintained schools, whilst the number of new entrants varied from 25000 to over 40000.[20]

A final influence on the supply of teachers may be called structural. The Secretary of State for Education can influence the number of training places. To some extent, if there are more places available, more people will apply and the supply of teachers will increase. This is particularly pertinent in the case of mature entrants to teaching. If there are colleges near home, many adults would like to train as teachers. The qualifications required for entry will also affect recruitment. If these are raised, then some people wishing to train will not be able to do so and the supply will show a corresponding fall.

Difficulties in Planning

Given the difficulties discussed above, it is not surprising that forecasts are less than accurate. Probably the most exhaustive investigation of the demand and supply of teachers was undertaken by the National Advisory Council on the Training and Supply of Teachers. In 1965 they forecast that the total number of qualified teachers in maintained schools would be 540000 in 1981.[21] The actual number was 470000.[22] Shorter term forecasts have also proved inaccurate, though closer to the actual, as might be expected. Even inaccurate forecasts may be useful, particularly if the alternative is leaving things to chance.

So far, the demand and supply of teachers has been discussed as if teachers were homogeneous and completely mobile. In practice this is not so, and difficulties arise because there are shortages of particular types of teacher or in particular areas, whilst numbers overall may be satisfactory. Table 5.1 gave the number of live births in England and Wales. The fluctuations shown there will affect different schools at different times. A fall in the birth rate will first affect nursery schools, then primary, secondary and further education in turn. Thus, it is quite possible for one sector to be contracting whilst another is expanding. Some teachers are happy to change sectors, but many cannot and so there may be a shortage of, say, primary teachers and a surplus of secondary.

Even in a particular sector there may be both shortage and surplus at the same time. Teachers of subjects such as maths and science may be needed by schools while there are plenty of teachers of other subjects available for employment. This has led to suggestions that teachers of maths and science should receive higher pay in order to attract more entrants – a suggestion opposed by teacher unions who do not wish to divide the profession. In fact differentials do exist. Zabalza *et al.* found that after standardising earnings for length of service, qualifications, sex and sector, mathematics graduates in 1971 earned on average 3.2 per cent more than other graduates and chemists 2.2 per cent more. Similarly, good honours graduates earned 9 per cent more than other graduates, who in turn earned an average 14 per cent more than non-graduates.[23] Such differentials do not eliminate the shortage, though in part this is because teachers with qualifications in mathematics teach other subjects.

An additional problem is spatial. The variations in birth rate will be greater in some areas than others and there will be population movement between areas. In new towns, for example, more teachers will be needed, whilst in declining areas there may be a surplus. Since teachers, like other workers, do not find it easy to move, these regional variations cause considerable problems both to planners and teachers.

A final difficulty occurs because of time lags. If the Secretary of State decides that more teachers need to be trained, then several years may elapse before they actually start work. As this is particularly true in the case of teachers who undergo four year training, it caused the Secretary of State in the 1970s to lay more emphasis on consecutive training – that is giving a one year teacher training to graduates. This reduced the time lags and made the work of the planners rather easier. What is less certain is whether the change was educationally desirable, for some teacher trainers believe that a degree plus one year's training is less suitable for primary education than a four year B Ed course.

References

1 Crowther-Hunt, Lord, 'The Inadequacies of Departmental Planning in Action', *Times Education Supplement*, 14 May 1976.
2 Williams, G., 'Educational Planning, Past, Present and Future', *Educational Policy Bulletin*, Vol. 7 No. 2, Autumn 1979, pp. 125–40.
3 David, M. E., *Reform Reaction and Resources: The 3 Rs of Educational Planning*, NFER, 1977, p. 208.
4 Carter, C., Ermisch, J., Ruffet, F., *Swings for the Schools*, Policy Studies Institute, Vol. XLV No. 584, December 1979.
5 DES, *Statistical Bulletin*, 2/82, January 1982.
6 Open University, *Providing the Teachers*, Unit 8 of Course E222, The Control of Education in Britain, 1979, p. 32.
7 *ibid.*, p. 33.
8 DES, *Statistical Bulletin*, 17/81, November 1981, Table 6.
9 Vaizey, J. and Sheehan, J., *Resources for Education*, Allen & Unwin, 1968.
10 International Labour Office, *Teachers' Pay*, Geneva, 1978, p. 90.
11 Standing Commission on Pay Comparability, Report No. 7, *Teachers*, (Clegg) Cmnd 7880, HMSO, 1980.
12 *ibid.*, p. 20.
13 Zabalza, A., Turnbull, P., Williams, G., *The Economics of Teacher Supply*, Cambridge University Press, 1979, p. ix.
14 *ibid.*, p. 3.
15 Lomax, D. E., 'A Review of British Research in Teacher Education', *Review of Educational Research*, Vol. 42 No. 3, 1972, pp. 289–326.
16 DES, Report on Education No. 78, *Teacher Turnover*, July 1973.
17 Zabalza, A., *et al.*, *op. cit.*, Figure 6.3.
18 Ollerenshaw, K., *Returning to Teaching*, Report of a Research Project, Dept of Educational Research, Lancaster University, 1973, p. 5.
19 Zabalza, A., *et al.*, *op. cit.*, p. 91.
20 DES, *Statistics of Education 1979*, Vol. 4, *Teachers*.
21 DES, *The Demand for and Supply of Teachers 1963–86*, Ninth Report of the National Advisory Council on the Training and Supply of Teachers, HMSO, 1965, p. 15.
22 DES, *Statistical Bulletin*, 14/81 1981.
23 Zabalza, A., *et al.*, *op. cit.*, p. 4.

6
Finance for Education

National Economic Policy

The finance needed to run the education system cannot be considered in isolation, for it is an important part of public expenditure, which is a crucial economic variable. If public expenditure is allowed to grow, it is probable that money spent on education will also rise: the converse is also true.

Decisions about the level of public expenditure depend in part on how well the economy is doing, for a booming economy can afford to spend more resources on public services. But that is not the whole story. Economic decisions are not taken in an intellectual vacuum, because no government can operate an economic policy without some kind of economic theory to guide it, even though this theory might not be made explicit and may even be implemented unconsciously. J. M. Keynes made this point in a famous passage:

> Practical men, who believe themselves to be quite exempt from any intellectual influences, are usually the slaves of some defunct economist.[1]

Until the Second World War, generally accepted theories caused governments to believe that what they could spend should be limited to what they received in tax. In other words, the budget should be balanced just as a family should try to keep its expenditure equal to or below its income. Excluding exceptional periods such as wars, the rule was that when the economy was booming governments would receive more in tax and could afford to spend more on public services such as education. When the economy was depressed, tax receipts would fall and governments should cut spending. Balancing the budget was thought to be not merely economically desirable, but became almost a moral duty.

This system of beliefs was largely overthrown by the work of J. M. Keynes, though elements of it still remain. Keynes's work has been so influential that some account of it is necessary if the formation of economic policy is to be understood. The ideas are often complex and any brief account is necessarily over-simplified. Keynes's major work was completed in the 1930s, and it is not therefore surprising that he was concerned to develop policies which would reduce unemployment. Keynes suggested that the prime cause of unemployment was insufficient aggregate demand. In other words, firms were forced to lay off workers because they could not sell the products they made; if demand for products could be increased so would employment. Consequently, Keynes argued that governments should manipulate aggregate demand so that unemployment was kept at a minimum, even if this meant a budget deficit.

However, aggregate demand is not easily managed, for it is made up of a number of components, some of which interact with each other and some of which are difficult to control. The largest component of aggregate demand is consumers' expenditure, which includes spending on services as well as consumer goods. This is largely influenced by the level of incomes in the community. Another component of aggregate demand is investment. In everyday life people use this word to include money placed in such places as building societies and unit trusts, but in economics the term is limited to spending on such things as factories, machines and raw materials, which help increase future production. Therefore, the level of investment depends on employers' expectations of future profitability, and hence on such factors as expected returns and the level of interest rates, for money must often be borrowed to finance investment. Exports form another part of aggregate demand, for if foreigners buy more of our goods, employment will increase. The level of exports is determined by several factors, most importantly by changes in the level of incomes in other countries and by the competitiveness of exporters.

So one thing becomes clear; these various components of aggregate demand are not easily controlled by the government. Fortunately, there is one other part of aggregate demand that is more easily influenced, and that is the government's own spending. If the government increases pensions or spends more on education, this money will increase demand and hence employment. However, even government's own spending is not that easy to control. Cuts are unpopular and take time to implement, whilst planned increases in spending may sometimes take several years to be effected, and have the further disadvantage that they commit the government to continuing increases in the future. Thus, if the government builds a new hospital, it will also be committed to future expenditure on staff and equipment.

These components of aggregate demand – consumption, investment, exports and government spending – are only part of the story, for they have to be balanced against other factors which reduce the level of aggregate demand. Thus, if people save more, they will have less to spend and demand will fall. This will also be true if people spend more on imports, for then the increase in demand will accrue to some other country. Taxes are yet another withdrawal from this system, for money taken by the government in tax reduces aggregate demand. On the other hand, if the government cuts taxes, they will tend to increase aggregate demand because people will have more money to spend.

So of all the variables in the Keynesian system, the two most open to influence are government spending and taxes. If the government is faced with high unemployment, it should increase aggregate demand by raising government spending and cutting taxes; if the major problem is inflation, the government should increase taxes and cut its spending in order to remove money from the system. In a Keynesian system the government should aim to use its taxes and spending to regulate the economy and not to balance the budget. The analogy that is sometimes used, which compares the government with a family, is false. A family which consistently spends more than its income will run into difficulties. A government which does this need not do so, for it can always borrow or create more money.

There are considerable practical problems involved in actually implementing this system. One difficulty is that the real world is immensely complex and the various factors interact with each other and with many other variables. Moreover, the relationships vary with time, so for example in some years people will save proportionately more than in previous years. This means that plans are always based on inadequate understanding of how the system operates. Moreover, measurement of the actual variables, such as investment, is inaccurate. Even if these difficulties are overcome there are long time lags in the system – statistics are out of date and the policy variables sometimes take a long time to be fully effective. For example, since many people pay income tax after the end of the financial year, a decision to raise taxation will involve a long time interval between the budget decision and the Inland Revenue actually receiving all the money. Moreover, a government's economic policy has more than one objective, and the measures which are appropriate for achieving one may clash with those necessary to achieve others. Thus, to improve the balance of payments a government may increase taxes and put up interest rates, so that consumers spend less on imports. However, these measures will also reduce aggregate demand and make unemployment worse.

Despite these problems, the Keynesian system was an important reason for the unprecedented prosperity experienced by many countries for thirty years after the Second World War. It is not clear whether economic problems in more recent years arise because of the inadequacies of the theory, or from external factors, such as increases in oil prices, or result from inadequate implementation of the theory. The Keynesian system has provided the rationale for most British economic policy and has had enormous influence on the level of government spending, and hence on the amount of finance available for education. Note that the theory does not demand any one level of government expenditure: those responsible for policy in a particular situation may be able to choose between a high or a low level of government spending if they vary other factors in the system such as taxes. Thus ministers' beliefs about the ideal size of government, or what tax levels are too high, will also influence the amount of money available for education. This was particularly important towards the end of the 1970s when a reaction against Keynesian methods occurred in Britain. One reason for this was the high inflation which seemed to some economists and politicians to be unresponsive to treatment by Keynesian methods. The rate of growth of the British economy was less than that of its competitors and this gave greater impetus to a surge of opinion in favour of new policies.

One main theme of these policies as proposed by Mrs Thatcher in Britain – and by President Reagan in the United States – was that government was too big. One argument was that public spending crowded out private enterprise, so that money and other resources were not available for businessmen seeking to invest. This argument found support in governments which ideologically supported the private rather than the public sector. The consequence of these beliefs was that public expenditure should be cut.

There was another closely related economic argument which led to the same conclusion. Put rather simply, the major problem in the economy was seen to be inflation, which one group of economists believed was caused by too much money in the economy, so the cure for inflation was to cut the money supply. It was believed that one reason for the excessive money supply was government borrowing; if this was cut, the money supply would tend to fall. Since governments borrowed to finance their spending, it was necessary to cut this in order to reduce inflation.

This account of how economic theories influence the level of public spending is oversimplified, but perhaps not unduly distorted. The important point is that the level of government spending is not determined by some objective analysis of 'needs', but by the perceived level of needs in relation to the growth of the economy and the ideological and economic perspective of the government.

Allocating Expenditure

In the financial year 1981/82, the total cash expenditure of central and local government was about £120 000 million. Allocating such a large amount to various purposes and controlling the spending, clearly involves considerable problems. The basis for the present system was a government enquiry, the Plowden Committee, which reported in 1961. This suggested that regular surveys should be made of public expenditure as a whole over a period of years ahead. Since that time the system has been varied in several ways. The planning procedures have grown increasingly sophisticated and the results are now published in a Public Expenditure White Paper.

Although the House of Commons is in theory responsible for deciding how much will be spent on various activities, the power actually resides elsewhere. The estimates that are sent to the Commons for approval are only rarely amended. The body which is primarily responsible for planning expenditure is called the *Public Expenditure Survey Committee* (PESC). This is an 'official' committee in the sense that it is made up of officials as opposed to politicians. Its chairman comes from the Treasury and it is essentially under Treasury control. The various spending departments, such as Education or Defence, submit estimates of expenditure not only for the coming year, but for the four or five years following. These estimates are based in part on the assumption that present policies continue, but they also contain bids for additional money to develop new programmes. The Treasury then negotiates with the departments, and clarifies the amounts of money involved; for example by inserting into the discussion a target figure for government wages and salaries during the following year. Since the bids for money always total more than the Chancellor thinks ought to be spent, the negotiations are long and difficult and involve not only the civil servants but also the ministers. Not infrequently these leak proposals to the press in order to summon up support for their policies. It is at this stage that strong ministers win more resources for their departments. The arguments are particularly fierce at times of economic crisis when existing policies have to be cut. The proposals eventually go to the Cabinet which, after several discussions in the full cabinet and in various committees, finally approves the plans. These are then published in a Public Expenditure White Paper which is debated and approved by the Commons. This process is repeated each year and in practice the various stages continue throughout the year.

PESC comprises elements of five processes.[2] The planning process includes not only a projection of the development of the economy over the next few years, but also resource plans for the spending departments and the costing and revision of plans. The allocating process decides between competing claims for available resources. The controlling process controls cash flows, ensures resources are committed by the spending authorities at the time stipulated and verifies the out-turn. There is also an evaluating function which compares intended and actual outputs and measures the impact of the outputs. Finally, there is an accounting process which not only audits the expenditure, but accounts to Parliament and the public.

The PESC system has many virtues. If the processes described above achieve their potential, then ministers should be able to control spending and to allocate it in an efficient manner. However, it is clear that there are difficulties with the system, and almost every year changes are made to try to improve it. One major problem is that it is extremely difficult to vary the level of public spending, especially in a downward direction. As Wright points out, the great bulk of public expenditure comprises current and capital expenditure on programmes which are resistant to change in the short run.[3] No government can cut the number of teachers employed next week, or close schools next term. Moreover, to increase or reduce current expenditure may require an Act of Parliament, which is time consuming and will certainly provoke political controversy because those suffering from the reduced expenditure are likely to protest. This is one reason why cuts are often made in the capital programme. This relates to the future and is therefore less unpopular, though concentrating changes on the capital programme may have considerable long term consequences, and it has severe effects on the construction industry.

Another problem is that forecasts are likely to be inaccurate. The total level of expenditure agreed in the Public Expenditure White Paper rests on assumptions about the performance of the economy as a whole, but this is affected by events outside the government's control, for example by the state of the American economy or by rises in oil prices. Changes in the economy as a whole will also affect particular sections; thus, if the economy falters, expenditure on unemployment will rise. Moreover, new policies take time to implement and are difficult to quantify, so that there is a tendency to overestimate rather than underestimate future expenditure.[4] This means that forecasts for the coming year may be inaccurate and that those for four or five years in the future will be very unreliable.

The problems of planning and control of expenditure are particularly difficult in areas such as education which are largely under the control of local authorities. What effectively is happening is that the government is saying that, given its reviews of likely resource and expenditure levels over the next few years, and accepting its ideas about priorities among the activities it would like to encourage, and those to which commitment has already been made, the figures represent what it would like to spend.[5]

Frequently, however, what the government would like to happen is not what the local authorities want to happen, and so the plans are not fulfilled. Moreover, as Hepworth points out, even though the public expenditure survey is important to local government, the implications of the survey do not in practice consciously affect the decision processes of local government for several reasons.[6] The most important of these is that it comes too late in the year to have any real effect on the spending decisions of the local authority for the following year. At present, local government does not regard itself as involved in the PESC process and does not consider itself committed to the results.

Despite all the problems, the PESC procedures remain the principle way in which government attempts to plan its future spending and to allocate its money to particular purposes.

Finance of Local Authorities

The gross expenditure of local authorities in 1980 was about £25 000 million. This huge total is financed in a number of ways. Most commentators suggest that about a quarter of the total comes from ratepayers, about a sixth from charges for rents and services, some from borrowing and interest receipts and a half from government grants. In fact, there are various ways to calculate the contribution of central government, and estimates vary from 60% to less than 40% if all local authority services are included.[7] Whatever the precise share, the amount of money involved is huge, and controversies are inevitable when this has to be shared among competing authorities. The position is made more complex because the different countries comprising the UK have varying systems. The account which follows is largely concerned with current spending in England.

Part of the grant from central government is for specific activities, for example to help a particular service, such as the police, or to help transport, especially public transport. However, most of the money is in the form of a general *Rate Support Grant* which is not allocated to a particular service. One part of the Rate Support Grant is the domestic rate relief grant, which as its name implies is intended to help domestic ratepayers. Thus if the local rate is 98 pence in the pound and the domestic rate relief rate is 18 pence, then domestic ratepayers will pay 80 pence, whilst other ratepayers such as shops and factories will pay the full 98 pence. This grant is in fact a device to reduce the enormous unpopularity of the rates.

Most government aid comes in the form of a block grant. The overall objective in the distribution of block grant is equalisation; that is, to enable all local authorities to provide a comparable level of service for a similar rate in the pound.[8]

Government help is needed because some areas have greater needs, and some are poor in the sense that they have low rateable values. Without government finance both these groups would have to set rates at a higher level in the pound to finance services equivalent to those in wealthier or less needy areas. An additional objective is that central government wants to be able to influence, if not control, the level of spending by local authorities and to constrain and discipline those individual authorities whose expenditure might be considered excessive.[9]

The mechanism for calculating the grant is complex, but essentially it consists of a comparison between the actual expenditure of a local authority and what the government thinks the authority ought to spend. An authority's entitlement to grant is the difference between its expenditure and what it can raise by applying a Grant Related Poundage to its own resources. This *Grant Related Poundage* (GRP) is set by the Secretary of State for the Environment and depends on the relationship between actual expenditure and *Grant Related Expenditure* (GRE), which is what the Secretary of State thinks the authority ought to spend. The system is organised so that if authorities spend much more than the GRE the grant is cut, thus penalising 'extravagant' authorities.

Calculation of the GRE is crucial to the system and a variety of methods are used. The amount of money an area receives depends in part on indicators such as the number of people and their characteristics, for example the number of old people and school children, the physical characteristics of the area and the extent of social and environmental problems such as bad housing. Analysis of past expenditure is also used. As the law allows changes to be made in the variables, local authorities do not know how much they will receive until shortly before their financial year begins. This means that they find long term planning very difficult and important financial decisions have to be taken very quickly.[10] In addition, the political complexion of central government can affect the system, for example Labour Governments may give more weight to indicators that help the inner cities.

There is always some tension in the relationship between central government and local authorities. Heclo and Wildavsky quote an official who claimed that 'all governments want to give local authorities more independence provided that the local authorities do what the Government wants them to do.'[11] To try to ensure that the local authorities do not exert too much independence there are a number of controls open to central government. The strongest of these is that the local authorities must be able to point to a specific statutory sanction for every act they undertake. In other words they cannot spend any money on any activity unless some Act of Parliament gives them specific authority to do so. Central government appoints auditors to check that local authorities do not exceed their powers and that money has not been spent 'unreasonably'. If the district auditor thinks that some item of expenditure is unreasonable (e.g., paying employees more than agreed national pay scales or refusing to increase council house rents) he can surcharge the councillors. This means that the councillors have to pay the unreasonable expenditure out of their own resources. As the amounts are often huge, it would often mean bankruptcy for the councillor. It is, therefore, a powerful deterrent to unorthodox or questionable expenditure.

Other controls can be analysed into several aspects:

1 Technical controls over the day to day running of services, for example by the inspectors of constabulary.
2 Making sure that authorities conform to national policies, for example to raise the school leaving age.
3 Control over the level of funds available to local authorities and to make it difficult for them to raise rates.[12]

In education some of these controls are direct and obvious, whilst some are more concerned with influence rather than control. The education service has been called a national service, locally administered. The 1944 Act gave the Minister of Education (now the Secretary of State) the duty 'to secure the effective execution, by local authorities, under his control and direction, of the national policy for providing a varied and comprehensive educational policy in every area.' In practice this 'control and direction' has been undertaken only in a very general way, with considerable discretion being left to local authorities. This leads Ranson to argue that 'education is more accurately described as a local school service occasionally administered from differential central positions such as the LEA and the DES.'[13]

Whilst the power is diffused throughout the system (including groups such as teachers and parents), there is growing concern that power is shifting from local authorities to Whitehall. This arises in education partly because government in recent years is taking an increasing interest in areas, such as the curriculum, which it formerly left largely to local authorities and schools. The concern is also felt in the area of finance. Over the last few decades the share of local government finance provided by central government has increased, and there is a widespread belief that 'he who pays the piper calls the tune'. This belief is reinforced by specific actions of central government such as the Local Government Planning and Land Act (1980), which introduced the block grant mechanism described above and which for the first time gave central government the power to penalise local authorities if the general level of expenditure was too high. Thus, it is claimed that legal obligations and central controls leave local education authorities only a small area of discretion. Items such as loan charges, the level of teacher and other salaries, and student awards, take up most of the budget, and local authorities cannot vary these items. The argument can be exaggerated. Hepworth shows that in the long run, the predilections of individual authorities can profoundly influence their patterns of resource allocation.[14] The evidence for this is clear from the substantial variations in the amounts spent by different local authorities on items such as secondary education or books. Moreover, there are a number of dimensions in central-local government relations which are often ignored. There are a variety of possible relationships depending on the resources available to local bodies, and on the influence of professional and political factors, so that it is possible to see the relationships in terms of a game where each 'side' has advantages and 'victories'. This leads

Rhodes to conclude that 'the "problem" of central-local relations is not, therefore, one of central control but of ambiguity, confusion and complexity . . . Ambiguity bestows room for manoeuvre. Freedom of action can be negotiated and renegotiated.'[15]

The debate is important because of the dangers of over centralised power. Jones puts forward a number of points to illustrate this. Services provided by central government may not suit local needs and conditions and may not reflect local wishes. If decision-making is centralised, there is less opportunity for public participation and individuals may become alienated as they recognise that decisions affecting them are taken by remote bodies scarcely accountable to them. Moreover, resources may be wasted if national policies are applied without variation to local need and local creativity and experimentation reduced, or ended.[16] If local government becomes just an administrative unit without real responsibility, then it is likely to behave irresponsibly. Local authorities will only be efficient and effective if they have the duty and the opportunity of raising a substantial part of the money they spend.

Local government receives its money from various sources. In addition to the central government grant, it receives income from charges such as rents or admission money to swimming pools, and it has the proceeds from a local property tax, 'the rate'. If local authorities are to run the same level of services but reduce their dependence on central government, it follows that they have to augment these by other sources of income. The search for alternative sources is strengthened by the great unpopularity of the rates.

There is no such thing as a perfect tax, but it is possible to suggest some criteria by which local taxes can be judged. Firstly, the yield should be appreciable and should be able to be varied as needs change. The tax should not be expensive to collect and the rate of tax should be under the control of local authorities.[17] Moreover, the tax should be 'progressive' – that is, those with higher incomes should pay proportionately more than poor people. It is this last criteria which seems to many people to be a failing of the rates system. There are many examples of people with low incomes paying high rates, and of households with high incomes paying little in rates. The Layfield committee of enquiry into local government finance examined the relationship between rate bills and income and found that its incidence was regressive; that is, the higher a household's income, the smaller the proportion of income it paid in rates. However, after allowance was made for rate rebates, the position was less clear, for the incidence of rates after rebate was progressive for those in the lower income groups, but the tax became regressive for those in the higher income groups who are not affected by the rate rebate system.[18]

The rates system also fails to satisfy some of the other criteria. Thus, while its yield is appreciable, it is not possible to increase this in line with rises in costs and changes in policy.

Whilst it is easy to find fault with the system of rates, it is not easy to find alternatives. Any alternative to rates must, on its own, or in combination with other taxes, be capable of producing a yield similar to that raised by domestic rates, provide each local authority with a potential yield sufficient to meet an appreciable part of its expenditure, and enable each taxpayer's liability to be determined with reasonable certainty in a way which commands general acceptance.[19] The Layfield committee did suggest that a local income tax might be introduced but it would be administratively very complex and would tend to favour areas whose residents had high incomes. Another suggestion is that local authorities should raise more money by charging for services where possible. They could raise some money by charging for services such as libraries, fire services, refuse collection and disposal and personal social services, as suggested by some writers,[20] but these would not raise appreciable amounts in relation to current local expenditure and they would be highly unpopular.

In 1981 the government issued a Green Paper entitled *Alternatives to Domestic Rates*. The paper discussed a number of possible alternatives to the present system, one of which was to remove the education service from the general government grant to local authorities, and instead give a grant specifically for education. This would force local authorities to meet a higher proportion of the cost of the remainder of local government services than they do at present, and 'Local taxpayers might then be more concerned that their elected representatives sought and obtained proper value for their money, with beneficial results for local authority efficiency.'[21] Another advantage claimed for this scheme is that it would encourage a greater consistency of service across the country. The strongest argument against this scheme came from those who believe in a local education service, and fear that a more specific government grant would mean much more central government control of education.

Allocation within Local Authorities

Once local authorities have been informed how much they will be receiving from central government grants, they can make firm plans for their own finances for the forthcoming financial year. Each local government department, such as education, will have drawn up continuance of service budgets – that is, a budget showing how much it expects to spend during the next year assuming no changes in policy. These might also include bids for additional sums of money, either to expand programmes or to introduce new ones.

These proposed budgets are then considered by one of the most important committees of the council, sometimes called the Finance or the Policy and Resources Committee. This has to total the proposed expenditures and balance this against income. Once the central government grant is known, they can calculate how much they would need to raise in rates and charges to balance their budget. As might be expected, there are strong pressures to cut spending and hence keep rates down. A period of bargaining takes place and the chairmen of spending committees try to obtain as much money as they can for their committees. The final decisions are made and the budget is sent to the full council for approval.

This brief outline conceals many of the difficulties inherent in the process. Local authorities find it very difficult to undertake long term planning because they do not know the government's intentions for particular services. Moreover they do not usually know how much money they will be receiving from central government grants until just before Christmas, and this gives them only a few weeks to plan their expenditure for the next financial year starting in April, and to steer this plan through the local government committee system. In the education committee for example, committee members will be faced with a budget document which itemises expenditure, sometimes in considerable detail. There is a real chance that members will be overwhelmed by the sheer volume of information so that most discussion concentrates on a few items which are of particular interest to only some individuals.[22] Thus any proposal to increase or decrease the number of staff will probably cause discussion and so will items which are seen as political. It is difficult, if not impossible, for individual councillors to vary the budget in a way that will improve efficiency or encourage effective planning, for they lack detailed knowledge and time to consider. Moreover, the final decision must not only meet what they believe to be the educational needs of the community, but also be acceptable to the Policy and Resources Committee and the full Council.

Finance for Higher Education

The source of finance for higher education varies according to the institution. A few institutions, such as the Open University and some voluntary colleges of higher education run by denominational bodies, receive direct grants from the Department of Education and Science.

These exceptions apart, there are two sectors of higher education. The local authority sector consists of institutions such as polytechnics, colleges of higher education and further education colleges in which higher education takes place. The other sector consists of self-governing universities.

British universities receive their finance from a variety of sources, but by far the most important of these is the University Grants Committee

(UGC) which supplies about three quarters of university income.[23] The rest comes from research grants, fee income and such things as income from catering. The UGC was established in its modern form after the First World War, and it was designed to provide public money to universities whilst preserving some independence from government control. It now exercises what could be fairly described as some control over the universities, and in recent years its role as a buffer has become weakened as government influence has increased.

For many years the recurrent grant to universities was settled on a quinquennial basis, but because of the problems arising from inflation and the need for economies this was suspended. In 1977–78 a new system was introduced whereby the grant was settled on a running four year basis, the sum for the first year being firm and the remainder indicative. The basic data used to calculate grants are the returns submitted by each university to the UGC showing its income and expenditure. The UGC assesses these in terms of unit costs and staff/student ratios, and considers policy factors such as a decision to give priority to science or engineering. The benefit of this approach according to the DES is that it enables actual outturns in expenditure and income to be monitored, and adjustments to be made as a result of any significant changes. The process also enables estimates to be made of the expenditure consequences of policy changes.[24]

The UGC system provided a method which was generally accepted within the universities when expansion was taking place. It became less popular when cuts had to be made in 1981, because the criteria on which these were based seemed to be unfair, with the decision based more on the subjective opinions of UGC members, rather than on objective criteria. This is not surprising as it is almost impossible to derive objective criteria that would be generally acceptable.

Public sector institutions of higher education have grown out of the old technical colleges that were administered by local authorities. However, higher education is extremely expensive, and if there was no system of compensation, those authorities with a large higher education sector would be subsidising those authorities which provided little or no higher education. Accordingly, a pooling system was set up. Each authority was required to contribute to the advanced further education pool an amount of money which would depend on its school population and its non-domestic rateable value. Thus an authority with a lot of children and many factories and offices contributed much more than those with few. In order to attain reimbursement from the pool, authorities sent to the DES annual statements of relevant expenditure on higher education.

The system became unpopular with several groups. The government disliked it because they had little or no control over the size of the pool. As the money involved is considerable – some £375 million in 1980–81[25] – this was obviously not acceptable to the Treasury. Many of the institutions found the system irksome. Large institutions, such as polytechnics, found that local authority control limited their autonomy and that their freedom to act was restricted by local authority education departments more suited to running schools. The local authorities wished to keep control of 'their' colleges, but found the costs large and the colleges arrogant. The dissatisfaction was easy to note, but the solution was less apparent. Almost all the parties involved believed that there should be a national body, perhaps similar to the UGC, but its precise composition and powers were less easy to agree.

In 1982 the government set up a National Advisory Body (NAB) for Local Authority Higher Education. The NAB was made up of a committee of local authority members under the chairmanship of the Minister for Higher Education, and a board with a wide membership from the polytechnics, the Department of Education and Science, and other institutions. This body was to advise the Minister on the development and finance of local authority higher education.

References

1 Keynes, J. M., *General Theory of Employment Interest and Money*, Macmillan, 1936, p. 383.

2 Wright, M., 'From Planning to Control: PESC in the 1970s' in Wright, M., ed. *Public Spending Decisions: Growth and Restraint in the 1970s*, Allen & Unwin, 1980.

3 *ibid.*, p. 94.

4 Else, P. K., and Marshall, G. P., *The Management of Public Expenditure*, Policy Studies Institute, Vol. XLV, No. 580, 1979.

5 Dennison, W. F., 'Expenditure Planning in English Education: Recent developments in the relationship between Central and Local Authorities', *Journal of Educational Administration and History*, Vol. XI, No. 1, January 1979, pp. 34–42.

6 Hepworth, N. P., *The Finance of Local Government*, Allen & Unwin, 6th ed., 1980, p. 40.

7 Crispin, A., 'Education and the Rate Support Grant, the case for a Block Education Grant', *Education Policy Bulletin*, Vol. 8, No, 1, Spring 1980, p. 1.

8 Heiser, T., 'RSG: Block Grant' in *Public Finance and Accountancy*, March 1981, pp. 13–15.

9 Crispin, A., 'The new Block Grant and Education – Central Control or National Direction', *Local Government Studies*, November/December 1980, pp. 25–37.

10 Bramley, G. and Evans, A., 'Great complexity causes controversy', *Municipal Journal*, 6 February 1981.

11 Heclo, H. and Wildavsky, A., *The Private Government of Public Money*, Macmillan, 1974, p. 334.

12 This list is partially derived from Hepworth, N. P., *The Finance of Local Government*, 6th ed. 1980, pp. 271f.
13 Ranson, S., 'Changing Relations between Centre and Locality in Education', *Local Government Studies*, Vol. 6, No. 6, November/December 1980, pp. 3–23.
14 Hepworth, N. P., *op. cit.* p. 203.
15 Rhodes, R. A. W., *Control and Power in Central-Local Government Relations*, SSRC, Gower, 1981, pp. 33, 34.
16 Jones, G. W., 'How to save Local Government' in *Town Hall Power or Whitehall Pawn*, Institute of Economics Affairs, 1980.
17 King, D. N., 'Local Government Finance and Autonomy' in *Town Hall Power or Whitehall Pawn, op. cit.* p. 23.
18 Layfield Committee, *Report of the Committee of Inquiry into Local Government Finance*, Cmnd 6453, HMSO, 1976, ch. 10.
19 *Alternatives to Domestic Rates*, Cmnd 8449, HMSO, 1981, p. 5.
20 King, D. N., *op. cit.*
21 *Alternatives to Domestic Rates*, *op. cit.*, p. 69.
22 Dennison, W. F., 'Expenditure Decision Making by English Local Education Authorities' *Education Studies*, Vol. 5, No. 3, October 1979, pp. 241–250.
23 Open University, *The Finance of Education*, Course ED322, Education Studies and Social Science, 1977, p.36.
24 DES 'Financial Model for Universities' Recurrent Grant', Minutes of evidence to the Fifth Report of the Education Science and Arts Committee, *The Funding and Organisation of Courses in H.E.*, Vol. 2, H of C 787 II, 1980.
25 *ibid.*

7
Issues in the Finance of Education

There is no ideal method of financing education. Every system has its advantages and disadvantages and the balance of argument changes over time. It would be quite possible to have a system with little or no state involvement, where the responsibility for obtaining an education belonged entirely to the individual. That was the situation which existed in most countries until just over a century ago. The advantage of this approach is that taxes could be much lower, and those without children would be considerably better off. The disadvantages are that this would place great burdens on families, and that there would be less education, so that ultimately the society would be poorer because of the contribution which education makes to economic growth and in its externalities. These disadvantages are so considerable that every state now provides or finances education on a massive scale.

However the problem remains: precisely how should education be financed and provided? This question is too large a subject to analyse here; what this chapter attempts is not to consider all possible alternatives, but to analyse briefly three issues which seem relevant and important today. Provision of student loans rather than grants, and the substitution of educational vouchers for state provision, are two ideas which have been advocated as alternatives to the present system, whilst the issue of equality in education has often been discussed but relatively rarely in its financial aspects.

Education Vouchers

Dissatisfaction with the existing system of financing education has led to a number of suggestions for change, and perhaps the most prevalent of these has been the provision of vouchers for education. This is not a new idea – West traces its origin back to Tom Paine's *Rights of Man*, though recent interest in the idea dates from the 1960s.[1]

The basic idea of a voucher is very simple. At present most education is not only financed by the government, but also provided by the government. A voucher system would change all this. In a voucher system, the government – either central or local – would issue a voucher to parents; the parents then take this to the school of their choice; the school returns it to the government and in return receives a cheque equal to the value of the voucher. Thus the government would continue to finance education, but the funds would go only to those schools in which parents chose to enrol their children.

There are in fact many differing voucher schemes – Maynard discusses eight varieties – though the differences are sometimes small.[2] The modern development of the idea is usually attributed to Friedman, an economist strongly committed to market forces as a means of allocating resources.[3] In a market system, consumer choice is supposed to decide what is produced. Thus if consumers start buying more small cars and fewer large ones, it will pay manufacturers to produce more small cars and fewer large ones. Firms which concentrate on small cars will make good profits, whilst producers of large cars will have to vary their product so that it satisfies consumer choice. Friedman and his supporters believe that market forces should be introduced into the education industry, so that schools produce the kind of education that consumers want.

In Friedman's version the value of the voucher is the same for each child, and it can be spent in any school that has been approved to take part in the system. This would include both private and publicly owned institutions. The schools could then charge supplementary fees if they so desired, making this system particularly attractive to private schools.

The most influential of the other versions is associated with the name of Christopher Jencks.[4] This scheme also makes use of market forces, and would encourage the provision of education by non-governmental groups, but it differs considerably from the Friedman model. Jencks and his colleagues supported the scheme because they wished to make radical changes towards control of the school by the community, rather than by the professionals. Furthermore they believe their scheme would help disadvantaged groups. In this system schools would not be able to accept additional payments, so schools accepting children from better-off families would not have greater income than those with a preponderance of children from poor families. Indeed the opposite would be the case, for children from poor families would receive a second, compensatory voucher which would be inversely related to income. In this way schools accepting poor children would receive additional finance.

Other voucher schemes have been less influential or contain variations on the above. The main questions of difference are (a) is the scheme open to private schools? (b) can the schools ask for additional money? (c) do poor or otherwise disadvantaged groups receive vouchers of higher value? Differences such as these mean that the effects of the schemes would vary substantially.

The most important argument put forward in favour of vouchers is that they would increase freedom of choice. This can be seen from the titles which proponents choose for their books: *Experiment with Choice in Education*[5] and *Education: A Framework for Choice*[6] are indicative of this. There is a widespread belief among economists, even those who do not necessarily support vouchers, that education is producer dominated in the sense that decisions as to curriculum, for example, are taken largely by teachers, and that parents can do little but respond to an existing situation. Teachers and educational administrators have only limited accountability.[7] It is argued that just as a market system provides the kinds of goods that the consumer wants, its extension to education would also force the providers of education to respond to the wishes of parents:

> Schools that cannot attract applicants will be faced with financial difficulties, possible closure, or take-over by more efficient management prepared to cater for the preferences of parents.[8]

Those schools which do provide the kind of education which people want will attract many pupils and hence more money to spend on teachers, equipment or even as profit. Vouchers would enforce the discipline of the market on the providers of education, just as it does on the producers of motor cars.

This belief in choice reflects a political view about the role of the state. Wiseman's views are typical:

> We postulate then a society which takes the freedom of the individual . . . as a prime social aim. In the economic sphere, this requires that individuals will be free in general to pursue their ends through a system of free exchange, with the functions of the state limited to providing the necessary legal background for enforcement of contracts, etc., to the prevention of coercion, to other measures necessary to keep markets free, and so on.[9]

In other words the state should only intervene in the market in very limited areas.

Closely linked to this interest in freedom of choice is the belief that vouchers will help to create a wider variety of school provision: '. . . one would expect to see schools emerging which reflect all kinds of cultures, aspirations and classes'.[10]

A closely related argument is that market forces involve competition and that competition encourages efficiency. There are several possible meanings of 'efficiency'. One is concerned with effectiveness, and supporters of vouchers argue that competition would lead to greater effectiveness on the part of schools.[11] This is because schools would have to provide more information to parents, and the need to define objectives and measure effectiveness would encourage schools to improve the level of achievement. Another view of efficiency is concerned with the allocation of resources. If schools had to compete as firms in private industry do, the inefficient ones would be forced out of business. Only the most cost effective schools would survive. Thus West comments: 'this system, because of choice and competition, promises a better quality of education for every pound already spent. . . .'[12]

West goes on to suggest another advantage: that a voucher system will allow more money to be spent on education, even in times of financial stringency. The argument is that if parents are allowed to 'top up' the value of the voucher provided from public funds, then the total amount spent on education will increase – assuming that the public sector contribution is not cut. In support of his argument West quotes the results of a survey which showed that many heads of households were prepared to supplement vouchers out of their own income.[13]

West claims that not only would this procedure ensure more money for education, it would also encourage greater equality of opportunity. This is because 'the real root of inequality of opportunity today lies in the inability of the lower income family to buy itself out of a bad school and into a good one.'[14] This inability would disappear if the state provided a voucher, for even lower income families would be able to afford a supplement. There is some disagreement between voucher supporters in this area. Those who support a Jencks type voucher do so believing it would lead to greater equality precisely because it would restrict the ability of the better-off to pay for a better education for their children, since under that scheme supplementary payments by parents would be prohibited.

There are numerous arguments against the introduction of vouchers. On the issue of choice, the claim is sometimes made that parents are not competent to choose schools, either because they are likely to be seduced by flashy marketing or because issues such as the curriculum are a matter for professionals. A related argument is that choice in education is limited by geographical factors in many areas. In rural areas there is often only one school within reasonable travelling distance. Moreover, in practice allowing choice to one parent may deny it for another. If parent A wants co-education and parent B chooses single sex education, these may be incompatible, for two small schools may be hopelessly uneconomic. The position is worse if parent C wants a Church of England school, parent D a Roman Catholic one, parent E a Moslem school. . . . Choice is limited in another way. If one parent chooses a private school for his child, then this makes it impossible to satisfy the choice of another parent who wishes for a school whose parents are representative of the community as a whole.

Wagner makes a number of critical points about choice.[15] He notes that all a voucher will do is to allow parents to state their preferences – if particular schools are over subscribed then the actual decision will be made by someone else. 'If a policy of increased parental choice is required, this can be provided for administratively without the need for a complicated system of vouchers'. The fundamental lesson about parental choice is that effective choice depends on resources. If there are sufficient resources to allow spare places in popular schools, then choice can be ensured without any need for vouchers. If there are no spare places, then a system of vouchers will not create them.

If vouchers do create additional resources for education, then more places may indeed be made available, but as Blaug points out, it is far from certain that a voucher system would necessarily raise total spending on education.[16] The classic argument for a social service wholly financed from tax is that the well-to-do and influential are encouraged to support high levels of expenditure; if this group are helped by a voucher system to opt out, then there will be less pressure on the government to provide more money. As inflation continues the government may fail to increase the value of the voucher in line with prices, thus cutting its value in real terms.

Opponents of voucher systems claim that they will lead to less social cohesion. This charge is made particularly of voucher systems which allow 'topping up' by parents. The private system of education in the UK is fairly small; if parents sending their children to such schools were subsidised, the sector would grow and British children would be more clearly divided into two nations. This splitting up would be reinforced by vicious and virtuous circles. The virtuous circle would exist in 'good' schools. These could attract parents not only willing to pay for their children's education, but who were able and eager to help their children's studies. These schools would therefore achieve good results in external examinations and consequently be even more attractive to parents keen for their children to succeed. The circle would thus continue. The vicious circle would exist in other schools. Those schools with a preponderance of children of low ability and/or low social class would achieve poor examination results and would not be able to charge extra fees. These poor examination results would drive away parents who placed great emphasis on examination success and the process would be reinforced. Schools would be more clearly divided than at present into 'good' and 'bad', and it would be particularly difficult to improve the latter. It must be noted, however, that these accusations would not apply to all voucher systems. Those which prevented supplementary payments by parents and which gave additional finance to children from poor families might increase social cohesion.

There are other objections to voucher systems. Teachers do not like the idea because it threatens jobs. Implicit in any system which uses market forces is the idea that those selling a successful product will be rewarded and those in less successful establishments will go to the wall. In the case of vouchers teachers working in schools which did not attract parents would be likely to lose their jobs. Moreover, a shift from public to private or a mixed public/private system will result in buildings and equipment in unwanted schools being left idle.

Empirical evidence

Whilst there has been considerable argument about vouchers there has been very little empirical testing of the ideas. In the late 1960s the American Office of Economic Opportunity developed an interest in vouchers and sought to initiate tests. They found considerable difficulty because the idea aroused opposition wherever it was suggested. Eventually one school district agreed to a trial. This was Alum Rock in the eastern section of San Jose, California. It would be hard to find a less representative area to test such a controversial idea. Approximately half the school children in Alum Rock are Mexican-American, 40% are Anglo and 10% are black. Most are from lower middle or lower class families and the population is highly transient with a 30% annual residential turnover.[17] One apt comment on this choice was that '. . . the voucher test thus began with one small and dusty California school district, poor and discontented'.[18]

The basic model used was that of Jencks with an extra compensatory voucher for poor children. There was to be a lottery system of admission to schools whose applications exceeded openings and free transportation for children enrolled at schools distant from their homes. Teachers' job tenure was guaranteed and each participating school would offer two or more distinct programme options, called 'mini schools', to ensure a wide variety of parental choice. The demonstration began with only six of the district's twenty four schools for young children agreeing to participate. From these emerged twenty two mini schools, and by the second year thirteen public schools were offering forty five programme options to parents.[19] One alternative private school (called 'Gro-kids') was organised by four young teachers. No parent selected Gro-kids and it promptly vanished.[20]

The experiment was extensively investigated by the Rand Corporation which received a grant for this purpose from the Office of Economic Opportunity. One of the claims made for vouchers was that it would ncrease variety in school. In Alum Rock great efforts were made to nform parents about the different programmes offered. However, lespite the use of mini schools, voucher schools turned out to be very imilar to non-voucher schools. The Rand Corporation researcher eported 'the model reveals that for Alum Rock, at least, the voucher ystem has not generated educational alternatives that are truly diverse . . the voucher classrooms are strikingly similar to the non-voucher lassrooms'.[21]

Another claim for vouchers was that it would transfer decision-naking power from the producers to the consumers; that is to the parents. In fact at Alum Rock the effects of experiment were limited because teacher tenure was protected. As the demonstration progressed the professionals changed the market aspects of the voucher scheme to suit their purposes, for example by making it impossible for schools to expand indefinitely to meet enrolment pressures. There was an increase in parent initiative – during the second year about 10% chose non-neighbourhood schools and after that the proportion rose to 18%. Cohen and Farrar conclude that 'the voucher demonstration appreciably increased parental choice among educational alternatives, but most parents failed to become more autonomous, powerful or involved'.[22]

Teachers experienced both gains and losses. Previously the curriculum had been set by central office staff, but as the scheme progressed there was an increase in the independence of teachers so that they had more control over the curriculum. The price they paid for this was a lot more work. There was 'an avalanche of meetings',[23] and even if their programme attracted more pupils they were not paid much more for their extra duties.

The Rand researchers were rather cautious in their analysis of the academic effects, but they suggest that the introduction of voucher schools seemed to make little difference to standards. For example, they found no appreciable or consistent differences in students' reading achievement between regular and alternative schools. They also found that parental choice was unrelated to student achievement and concluded that 'the justification for implementing alternative education programs probably should not be based on the promise of enhanced student outcomes'.[24]

Any conclusions derived from Alum Rock must be tentative, partly because one cannot generalise from one experiment, partly because that experiment was in such an untypical area. On the positive side, parents were more satisfied and had more choice of schools. However, these gains cost a good deal in financial terms, and instead of an increase in power to parents, the professionals gained in this respect. On the whole the results of the experiment do not support either the great hopes or fears expressed in the arguments about vouchers.

Vouchers in the UK

Voucher enthusiasts in the UK have not had the opportunity to initiate an experiment, though they have undertaken a feasibility study.[25] This took place in the Ashford division of Kent, an area with fifty two maintained schools and a population of 81 000. The education system in that area is organised so that at the age of eleven pupils transfer to high schools, normally the one nearest their home, though there is an appeals procedure for dissatisfied parents. At thirteen some pupils transfer to an upper school as a result of 'guided parental choice', and there is a procedure for judging cases where parent and authority do not agree. The system seems to provide a good deal of satisfaction with allocation. Over 95% of parents got their first choice of school at eleven and there were only about ten appeals per year against the thirteen plus choice of school.

The Kent investigation made extensive use of questionnaires and interviews. Parents were asked which school they would send their child to if they had a voucher, and about 13% indicated a different school from the one now attended by their child. If they could use the voucher at private schools, 17% of parents in social class I would move their child from a maintained to a private school. The figure was much less for those from lower social classes.

Teachers were also questioned and expressed strong opposition, though this was partly prompted by advice from the teacher unions. Half the teachers said they would refuse to teach in voucher schools, though doubtless this figure would fall if it came to the crunch. The strongest support for the scheme came from the private schools, all of which said they would be prepared to take part in voucher schemes so long as they maintained control over entry.

The financial aspects of a voucher scheme were also analysed. The costs varied from just over £90 000 a year for a limited scheme – mainly for administrative expenses – to nearly £2 million if private schools were included and poor children were given supplementary vouchers. This higher figure would be reduced if teachers in the maintained sector were made redundant as pupils transferred to the private sector.

The financial difficulties in the scheme can be illustrated if particular schools are studied. The major item in school costs is teacher salaries and these vary considerably from school to school, partly because pupil-teacher ratios differ, but also because some schools have more teachers at the top end of the salary scale. If the voucher was made to equal the average cost per pupil in the entire system, those schools with young teachers and a high pupil-teacher ratio would have large sums available to spend on other items, whilst schools with an ageing staff and low pupil-teacher ratio would not be able to pay their salary bill.

Consideration of loan charges introduces an even more inequitable element, for whilst old schools have little or no loan charges outstanding, new schools have considerable debts.

There is thus great difficulty in providing every school with equal residual income for each child. If the two items of salary and loan charges were removed, the resulting voucher would only be worth £44 for primary children and £83 for secondary (in 1977–78). These small sums hardly constitute a substantial delegation of resources from County Hall.

The investigation concluded:

> the general impression that emerges from responses to this inquiry is that choice of schools is seen as vital by parents, but that vouchers

would not necessarily be the only or the most satisfactory means of achieving it. Freedom of choice, the full information about schools necessary for such choice, the right of transfer between schools and subsidised transport where necessary to the chosen school – these are the critical elements. The decisive factor in making them possible, with or without vouchers, would be the availability of surplus capacity in the schools.[26]

Overall the voucher debate has been stronger on argument than on evidence. What does seems to emerge from both Alum Rock and Kent is that relatively few parents would take the opportunity to move schools – that the ability to do this depends on spare places and that more parental choice could be obtained without a voucher scheme. Even if it was introduced, power would tend to remain with the professionals and not devolve on to the parents. The system would involve additional expense for relatively few benefits. The disadvantages might be considerable, particularly if parents were permitted to supplement the voucher. As Levin points out:

> the voucher approach would violate the underlying premises of schooling in a democratic society. By segregating students in school environments that tend to reinforce values, prejudices, attitudes and behaviours of their parents, the diversity of experiences and exposure to other viewpoints, which are at the base of the democratic process, will be largely eliminated from schools. . . . To a large degree public support will be utilized to provide education outcomes that conflict with the social purpose of schooling.[27]

Student Loans

The Case for subsidy

It is not self-evidently true that government should subsidise higher education. Those teaching in this area tend to have pleasant working conditions and adequate incomes. Those who are students generally have an enjoyable life style and good financial prospects. There are, however, valid reasons for state subsidies.

Educationally, the purpose of subsidies is to make it possible for the most able students to enter higher education irrespective of their financial background. Similarly, there are social reasons deriving from either a belief in a more equal society or in greater equality of opportunity. It is generally accepted that higher education should not be denied to anyone simply because of their poverty. This reason gains added force because higher education is associated with higher earnings and therefore restricting access of poor people would perpetuate and reinforce existing inequalities.

There are a number of economic arguments for subsidies. It is generally accepted by economists that the state should provide – or finance – so called 'public' goods, where the benefits are spread indiscriminately and do not benefit any individual. The classic example of this is defence; if the country is adequately defended this is to the benefit of everyone in the country. It is sometimes argued that education is a public good, but it is clear that not everyone benefits equally from expenditure on higher education. The benefit goes primarily to those who are educated. The case for public subsidies therefore depends on the existence of external or spillover benefits which accrue to others. Examples of externalities for higher education are that it leads to a more civilised society, and that it encourages developments such as scientific knowledge and faster economic growth which raise incomes for the rest of society. These externalities cannot be measured and do not indicate what *level* of subsidy would be appropriate.

There is a rather different economic argument. If higher education was a good investment, it could be suggested that banks and other financial institutions would provide loans to students just as they do to businesses. In practice they are reluctant to do this because students lack collateral. The educational investment exists in the student's head and cannot provide security as do bricks and machines for loans to businesses. Because of this failure of the capital markets, it is argued that the government should provide some sort of security so that financial institutions are willing to lend to students.[28]

These reasons do not suggest either the level or the form of government subsidy. At one extreme the government could provide no aid to higher education except perhaps guaranteeing loans to poor students. At the other extreme it could pay not only the full cost of the education but also all the living costs for all students. Moreover there are many different methods of subsidy, including the provision of vouchers to students,[29] direct subsidy to institutions, direct subsidies to some or all students, or the provision of cheap accommodation or part-time paid employment.

The current position in the UK is that institutions of higher education are subsidised either directly, or through the University Grants Committee, or via local authorities. Students are also subsidised directly because those on designated full-time courses (including not only those courses leading to a degree but also higher diplomas of TEC and BEC) are legally entitled to a mandatory award. The awards are means-tested, with the parental contribution being assessed on a sliding scale after allowance has been made for deductions for such things as mortgage interest. There is a minimum award which covers fees and a small cash sum. Those who support the introduction of student loans argue that the present system is unsatisfactory, but there is less agreement about the precise form that loans ought to take. In the USA quite a wide variety of systems have been suggested or are in operation. The most notable of these include loans from private sources such as banks, where repayment is guaranteed by the government; direct loans of various kinds by the government; and income tax relief, so that parents may deduct fees from their income tax payments.[30] In the UK the differences between the schemes usually concern the extent of the loan and the method of repayment. Mishan, for example, favours a full cost loan scheme. Thus students would be required to repay all tuition costs including capital costs.[31] Peacock and Wiseman favour a voucher scheme to cover tuition costs with a loan scheme to cover student maintenance.[32] This would be repaid by borrowers adding to their income tax payments a sum equal to a specified percentage of his or her taxable income. Thus graduates who earn high incomes would pay more than those who earn low incomes. Schemes which make repayments depend in some way on 'ability to pay' are usually called income-contingent. As incomes usually rise with age, such schemes tend to have low repayments in the early years and higher repayments in later years when salaries are higher. These income-contingent loans have many features of a proportionate tax on graduates' income, and some people have suggested that instead of a loan scheme a graduate tax should be introduced.[33] This differs from a loan scheme in that participation would be compulsory and that the tax would be payable over the whole working life, rather than for a set period as with most loan schemes. There are, therefore, many varying loan schemes and the precise effects of each would vary. Nevertheless, it is possible to discuss the possible advantages and disadvantages of such schemes in general terms.

Arguments for and against loans

One advantage claimed for loans is that they could allow governments to cut public spending or alternatively provide more money for higher education. Thus Glennerster *et al.* argue that a graduate tax 'would help to ease the constraint on educational expenditure'.[34] In times of economic difficulty money provided from repayments would provide a cushion against government cuts. If governments did not cut expenditure, then the additional finance provided by loans would help to increase the provision of higher education. A related claim is that the impact on local government finance would be considerable and beneficial.[35] Public sector institutions of higher education provide a heavy burden on local government finance and, depending on the scheme, loans would reduce or remove this burden.

On the other hand critics suggest that the savings to government would only be small, since the government would still have to provide money for loans now and would only be repaid over many years. Thus, in the short run, the savings would be almost non-existent, though the cost would fall on different people, since subsidy of students through loans ultimately imposes a smaller burden on the general taxpayer than subsidy through outright grants.[36]

Another argument put forward by supporters of loan schemes is concerned with equity. Maynard claims that:

> the student may be relatively poor whilst he is studying but over his life his earnings are above average. These enhanced lifetime earnings could be used to repay the costs, at present met largely by taxpayers who may earn less than the average, of higher education.[37]

Similarly Mishan claims that the existing British system is one 'under which the underprivileged working class is, in effect, compelled to finance the education of the well-off majority of students'.[38] Opponents of loan schemes are also concerned with equity. Their principle is that no one with the ability to benefit from higher education should be barred from doing so because of poverty. Decisions about education are often made by parents, and working class parents in particular would be reluctant for their children to take on a large debt. The proportion of working class children in higher education is already low; a loans scheme would reduce even this. To this argument the supporters of loans suggest that there is need for careful investigation of the motivation of working class children, but they point out that working class children are filtered out of the higher education 'cohorts' as early as primary school, and that any disadvantage to this group could be overcome by offering a differential subsidy to them.[39] This of course could also be done by a modification of the present grants system. Moreover, the fact that the recipients of grants are being subsidised for an activity which will probably increase their earnings is no more an argument against grants than the fact that the owners of businesses benefit by the subsidies and tax incentives given to promote investment. The question to ask is: is the subsidy effective?[40] The argument about working class children is in fact just one aspect of the effect which a loans scheme might have on the demand for higher education. Critics suggest that there would be a fall in student numbers, leading to empty places in institutions of higher education, and which would make worse the low proportion of students in British higher education compared with other countries.

Another argument in favour of loans is concerned with efficiency because 'they would give the consumer (the student) the power to penalise inefficient producers (universities, polytechnics and colleges of education) by withdrawing'.[41] This is a curious 'advantage' to claim, not only because it would seem to penalise the student more than the institution, but also because the present system of grants allows students to change courses and even institutions. If university income was derived entirely by fees paid or by borrowed money, the impact on the institution would be greater, but so would be the effect on the student.

The efficiency argument can be developed in other ways. If students borrow money, they may be better motivated to work. If institutions derive their finance directly from the customer, they would have stronger incentives to innovate and put on courses relevant to the perceived needs of the students. To this claim opponents of the scheme maintain that the British higher education scheme is, in comparative terms, highly efficient. This is not only because British degree courses are shorter than those in other countries, but also because the student drop-out rate is lower.[42] If students faced financial difficulties resulting from loans, so that they resorted to an increase in part-time work, the result might well be lower academic standards and a higher drop-out rate.

If a loans scheme were introduced a number of difficulties would have to be overcome. The first of these concerns what is sometimes called 'the negative dowry problem'. The Robbins Committee suggested that the introduction of a loans scheme might lead to fewer girls entering higher education, or that the eligibility for marriage of the more educated girls would be diminished because they would take with them into matrimony not only a degree but also a debt.[43] This problem has often been exaggerated. Not only would few men refuse to marry a girl because she had a debt, but women graduates earn more than other women and are more likely to be working. In any event, the problem can be mitigated by exempting the mothers of young children from any repayments.

A more serious difficulty, as even proponents agree, is what to do about graduates who emigrate. It would be impractical to enforce collection on the basis of foreign earnings, though it might be possible to collect a lump sum from emigrants at the time of departure, or to conclude international agreements, at least with some countries, to ensure repayments. It seems likely that such schemes would not only be administratively difficult but would also be impractical. Although the supporters of loans claim that since no money is recouped from emigrants at present a loan scheme would not make things worse, this is not true. If graduates working in the UK had to repay the loan whilst those who emigrated could avoid it, the result would be an increase in the likelihood of emigration. Since graduates would 'incorporate' a large amount of public money even under a loans scheme, the result would be a loss to the country. A related problem is posed by defaulters. The administrative costs of chasing up individuals who deliberately or inadvertently ceased repayment – or who never commenced repayment – might be considerable.

Empirical evidence

Whilst one must be cautious about applying overseas experience to the UK, it is possible to draw some possible conclusions. Extensive use is made of loan schemes in several countries in Europe, in the USA and Canada and in Japan and Latin America. As might be expected the schemes vary considerably from country to country, but there do seem to be some common factors. In most countries the rate of interest is well below the commercial rate and very few of the schemes are self-financing. In some countries, such as Sweden, the costs of administration are low and the proportion of graduates who default upon their loan repayments is also low.[44] Experience in the USA has been less happy, and lenders have had to cope with a high incidence of default among student borrowers, as well as with numerous discharges of student loans in bankruptcy proceedings. Thus the Guaranteed Student Loan scheme had 334 000 defaulters as of June 1977, and in 1979 losses to the schemes by graduates becoming bankrupt totalled over $10 million.[45]

The introduction of a scheme for student loans would undoubtedly raise opposition, though one survey of opinion suggests that such an act would not have deterred many students from enrolling. Moreover the general public expressed support for loans, and the authors of the survey suggest that a judicious proposal to introduce a loans scheme would not be opposed by students and their parents to anything like the extent which might be suggested by the predictable opposition of students' representatives.[46] However, that is not the crucial point. A system of loans would not reduce government spending by any substantial amount unless students were expected to pay tuition costs. Most damaging of all, it would shift the British system of higher education in the direction of greater inequality.

Education and Equality

The financial activities of government can affect the distribution of income in two main ways. The most obvious of these is through its tax system. Taxes which bear more heavily on the rich, such as capital gains tax and income tax, lead to greater equality of resources in society. Not all taxes do this; for example, taxes on cigarettes and beer may affect some poorer sections of society particularly strongly. But taxes are only part of the story. Government spending also affects the distribution of income, especially if 'income' is defined to include not only money but consumption of resources. Thus if government spends more on such things as unemployment pay, social centres for the blind, free school meals for poor children or old age pensions, then the poorer sections of the community will benefit. On the other hand, if government allows high mortgage interest payments to be claimed against tax, gives subsidies to 'public' schools or to 'private' hospitals, then the effect will be to benefit some better-off sections of society.

The net effects of government taxation and spending are extremely difficult to analyse. For example, who benefits from government spending on defence, research grants, or the fire service? However, it is possible to make comments about the redistributive effects of some items of expenditure. Direct transfers of cash, such as pensions, redistribute income in favour of the less well-off. Benefits from services such as health tend to depend on such factors as the age composition of the household, so families with old or very young members tend to benefit. Some services, such as the provision of libraries, museums or the subsidies of classical music, tend to benefit the middle class. The overall effect is difficult to estimate precisely. The Royal Commission on the Distribution of Income and Wealth calculated that the overall effect of taxes and government spending was to reallocate resources from the better-off sections of the community to the less well-off; in other words to increase income equality in the country. The effect varied with the size of family, for large families benefitted, whilst childless ones tended to lose.[47] Because of the difficulties in their composition, such estimates can only be tentative and in any case do not necessarily reflect the quality of the services received. Thus, for example, better-off families may receive better quality service from doctors or teachers.

In any case the actions of government through its taxes and spending may exacerbate or reduce the impact of other forces which influence the distribution of incomes. Apart from education, these other factors include personal characteristics such as ability and luck, parental influences such as social class, which are associated with high income for their children and of course there is a link between parental wealth and child's later earnings.

The influence of schooling on earnings is the subject of some controversy. A major review of the evidence was carried out in the USA by Jencks. He concluded that reform of schools could not be expected to bring about significant social changes outside the schools, and in particular that equalising educational opportunity would do little to make adults more equal.[48] Jencks' work has been criticised on a number of grounds. It is claimed that he underestimates the effects of education because he is only concerned with income inequality, which is a very partial and inadequate measure of inequality.[49] Moreover, he ignored factors such as age and job experience and fluctuations in earnings. From a policy aspect it is also claimed that whilst policy may not be very effective in reducing inequality between individuals, it can have a substantial effect in reducing differences between groups.[50] Other writers have concluded that school does make a difference. Thus Psacharopoulos finds that education is significantly related to earnings, with length of education being the crucial factor.[51]

The classical liberal belief is that social mobility will be promoted by equal opportunity of education. The roots of this belief can be traced to writers such as Rousseau, who claimed that in the 'natural' state men were born equal and personal qualities would not jeopardise social equality so long as society rewarded people according to their merits. Thus the writers of the American Declaration of Independence could claim that 'all men are created equal', in the sense that they were born with the same moral and political rights. It follows from this belief that social institutions such as education should in some sense attempt to treat people equally. This view has been particularly strong in the USA where the school was seen not only as the institution which civilised the west and turned immigrants into citizens, but which also provided a common experience for all, so that the great nineteenth century American educator Horace Mann could call education 'the great equaliser'.[52] Evidence in favour of this belief is mainly in the form of case studies. There are innumerable examples of people from poor families who have taken advantage of educational opportunities and proceeded to obtain better jobs and higher incomes than they would otherwise have done. If the state did not provide education without charge, these individuals would have been denied the opportunity for advancement. There is also some statistical evidence to suggest that in the USA wage differentials have narrowed, indicating that education may play a part in equalising income, and some research does indicate that more schooling is positively related to improved income distribution.[57]

As Husen points out, the liberal vision of equal opportunity prevailed in most Western industrial countries until the late 1960s. There was a widespread belief that by removing economic barriers and making more places available in upper secondary and higher education, and by increasing the length of attendance in the common school, ideal conditions could be created to implement the vision of equal opportunity, where everybody had access to the kind and amount of education that suited his inherited capacity.[54] During the 1970s the economic and political context of education changed, which led to growing scepticism concerning the contribution made by education to equality. Thus Johns and Morphet claim that: 'Differences in income in a society of illiterates are far less than among individuals in an ordered society such as the United States'.[55] Whilst this may be true, it does not follow that the causal factor is education. However there is rather more precise evidence. Thurow points out that in the years between 1950 and 1970 in the USA there was a substantial movement in the direction of greater equality of education, but the distribution of income became less equal.[56]

In the UK a rather different approach was undertaken by Halsey *et al.* who used life histories of a national sample of 10 000 men aged twenty to sixty four in 1972. They found that the proportion of grammar school children from all classes went on increasing right up to the mid-point of the century, the relative rates being highest for the working class, but the absolute increases being highest for the middle class. Subsequently, what the working class gained from the expansion of the grammar schools, they largely lost through the decline of the technical schools. Over the period as a whole those born into professional and managerial families had three times as much spent on them as those born into the families of agricultural labourers. Educational spending helped maintain class inequality, particularly spending on higher education.[57]

There are a number of reasons which explain this kind of result. The educational system is there to impart competencies, and therefore almost by necessity creates differences. Moreover, as Husen points out, in widely different social orders, those who 'made it' to advanced positions (not least by means of advanced education) tend to pass on their privileges to the next generation.[58] Thus the children of the middle and upper classes tend to stay on at school longer than those from less privileged sections of society. In their analysis of educational spending in the UK between 1920 and 1965, Vaizey and Sheehan pointed out that one of the most important developments was that there had been a major switch towards expenditure that directly benefits those that stay on at school, in other words to the higher income groups.[59] This suggests that the provision of education by the state might actually be encouraging greater inequality by providing more resources to the better-off.

There have been a number of studies of the provision of education related to equality both in the UK and in the USA. Guthrie analysed spending in Michigan and concluded that less money was available from local sources for the schooling of low socio-economic status students than was the case for those of high status.[60] A later work, edited by him, points out that comparison between states was difficult because the basic data was not comparable, but that there seemed to be more disparity in populous states and in those with many school districts.[61] Another American study, by Johns and Morphet, suggests that states with the highest income spend more per head on their childrens' education; that children in these states stayed on longer at school and were less likely to fail the mental tests in the national service draft.[62] In recent years the American courts have ruled that states should attempt to equalise resources. The evidence suggests that this is difficult to achieve, and that even if differences between districts are reduced, those within districts will remain.[63]

In the USA the federal government provides relatively little money for education. Though some of this does attempt to equalise resources, in general federal funds flow in a fashion that permits high socio-economic and wealthy districts to receive an allocation of federal money per pupil equal to or greater than that received by low socio-economic and poor districts.[64]

In the UK clearly there are observable differences in wealth between districts but it might be argued that as a high proportion of spending by local authorities comes indirectly from central government, this would reduce differences in spending. However, the evidence suggests that this is not so. Eileen Byrne analysed the availability and allocation of resources in three local education authorities over the period 1945 to 1965. She concluded that the combination of basic inequality of resources in the 1940s, and of subsequent discriminatory education planning of 'rationed' buildings, financial and staffing resources, created a cycle of deprivation which was reinforced over the years. This cyle of deprivation was most evident for secondary modern pupils in small schools in the poorer authorities. She suggests that there was a direct correlation between the low rate of investment in the non-grammar schools (poorer buildings, less generous staffing, and lower equipment allowances) and their lower achievement on leaving school which was not accounted for by lower ability.[65] Byrne's points about poor buildings are supported by Taylor and Ayres. Their research suggested that government control of capital expenditure on schools meant that funds were directed so that new schools were provided for children in expanding areas, leaving relatively little money for replacing old schools in the poorer declining areas. They concluded that the system of finance meant that two nations were growing up. Those from favourable environments attended well equipped and well staffed schools; those from deplorable environments went to obsolete schools.[66]

This conclusion receives support from a study of an individual London borough. Tunley *et al.* analysed provision in Newham. They found that in 1973–74 there was little consistent relationship between social conditions and provision in schools, but by 1976–77 the most socially advantaged children (measured by indicators such as household amenities and unemployment) received the most favourable level of resources.[67]

Another investigation in this area was undertaken by Byrne, Williamson and Fletcher. They analysed data from almost all the local education authorities in England and Wales. The variables were concerned with local authorities' policy, local environmental factors, class background, provision and attainment. Their results indicate a clear interconnection among these areas, emphasising what the authors' term 'the absence of territorial justice in education in this society'. For example, one area analysed was staying on rates beyond sixteen. They found that poor areas were associated with low attainment and low staying on rates.[68] Their results have been questioned on a number of grounds. It is argued that the adoption of egalitarian policies is not associated with improved attainment and that their statistical methodology was unsatisfactory because they used aggregate data.[69] The difficulty of coming to generally acceptable conclusions in this area arises in part because policies change, because there are so many variable interactions and because the researchers' political beliefs may affect their conclusions. Above all there is the problem of determining causation. Statistical correlations do not prove cause and effect. Nevertheless it seems fairly clear that children from better-off areas tend to stay on at school longer and have more money spent on their education from public funds than is spent on the children of the poor.

In higher education the disparities of provision are much clearer, though international comparisons are difficult because the term 'higher education' covers a variety of institutions and courses so that the concept of average expenditure per student in higher education is almost devoid of meaning. Nevertheless empirical studies in a number of countries support the assertion that middle class students benefit handsomely from the system.[70]

The reason for this is that 'free' education is likely to have the opposite effect to that which is generally assumed. In practically every country in the world higher education is heavily subsidised by the state on the grounds of equal access, but those actually entering higher education are more likely to come from the better-off sections of society, partly because they can afford private preparation for entry and the indirect cost of earnings foregone whilst the student is still at school. Psacharopoulos analysed data from sixty four countries and found that university students are very heavily subsidised in poor countries, yet it is in these countries that access to higher education is particularly restricted.[71] One solution to this may be the extension of lifelong education. However, experience so far suggests that those who take advantage of educational opportunities are precisely those who have received most education. Efforts to shift resources into post-initial education for disadvantaged groups such as the unemployed may 'offer a continuing pseudo education for the havenots and still more education for the haves'.[72] This is because non-educational factors may easily subvert the intentions of educational engineering.

There is substantial regional inequality in England and Wales. McDowell shows that almost twice the proportion of eighteen-year-olds brought up in the south east go to university compared to those from the north of England. There are considerable variations in the supply of university places, with more places being available in the areas with a high proportion attending university. Social class differences remain important, for in the early 1970s the chances of going to university for those children born in 1953–54 to fathers in professional employment were nine times greater than those for children of manual workers.[73] As university education is the most expensive part of the education system, this means that the method of financing higher education involves spending more money on the children of the middle class than on the working class. As the middle classes tend to be better off, this means that the state spends more to educate the children of the wealthier sections of society.

Policy

It is, of course, open to argument whether or not the state should adopt a policy of seeking greater equality. West argues that the notion of equality of opportunity is as elusive a philosophical idea as it is a practical target,[74] whilst Lucas claims that to speak of equality in education is rather like speaking of equality in love. Learning or teaching are like loving and friendship in being primarily a matter of personal initiative and personal responses.[75]

In part differences of opinion arise because there are considerable differences in definition. Garms *et al*. suggest that equal opportunity can imply equal access to education, equal educational treatment or equality of educational outcome.[76] Each of these would require differing policies for their achievement. Bowman goes further and lists seven diverse definitions of equity in the provision of education. Some of these are fanciful (ensuring each individual reaches his full potentialities or ensuring proportional representation from every ethnic, social status, sex or other relevant category).[77] Clearly equity expressed in these terms cannot be achieved, though it may prove a useful goal. It is clear therefore that there is not one generally accepted definition, and indeed particular definitions may reflect the author's political orientation so that an elitist orientation might restrict the notion of equality of opportunity to a certain top per cent of the ability range.[78]

If the definition of equity that is accepted is one of a direction rather than a precise place, and if this is seen in terms of provision of resources, then certain policies will be likely to lead towards greater equity. Johns has outlined the characteristics of an equitable school finance programme, and whilst his points are not always applicable outside the USA they are indicative of one line of thought. The main points are:

1 Finance should be available to guarantee each student programmes appropriate to his needs and equal to those provided to similar students elsewhere.
2 The quality of education should not depend on the wealth of the district in which he lives, nor on the willingness of the electorate to raise local taxes.
3 The finance programme should allow for special educational activities needed by some but not all students such as the handicapped or exceptionally gifted.
4 Extra finance should be provided where costs are higher as in very rural areas.
5 An equitable system should also allow for innovation, be based on an equitable tax system, and utilize objective measures in allocating funds to local districts.[79]

Halsey suggests rather more radical policies. He claims that it is not enough to substitute flat equality for the present unequal reinforcement of advantages already distributed to families in a hierarchy of class and status. The system should 'follow the principle of positive discrimination directed against all arbitrary or accidental, and therefore unfair, disadvantages. This would mean less for the universities and more for the nurseries, less for Solihull and more for Newham, less for the eighteen to twenty-one-year-olds and more for the over sixty-fives'. There would be a right to time free from work. Education would take place in community schools and higher education would become adult education.[80]

Such policies are controversial and perhaps impossible to implement because of the opposition they would create. Halsey's points go beyond the scope of the economics of education and into the wider aspects of the whole structure of society. This is clearly necessary if there is to be substantial progress towards a more equitable system, for education is an integral part of the whole organisation of society. In a hierarchical society, it is inevitable that the education system will also be hierarchical.

References

1 West, E. G., 'Tom Paine's Voucher Scheme for Public Education' *Southern Economic Journal*, Vol. 33, January 1967, pp. 378–82.
2 Maynard, A., *Experiment with Choice in Education*, Institute of Economic Affairs, 1975, p. 27f.
3 Friedman, M., *Capitalism and Freedom*, University of Chicago Press, 1962, Ch. 6.
4 Jencks, C., *et al.*, *Education Vouchers: A Report of Financing Elementary Education by Grants to Parents*, Centre for the Study of Public Policy, Cambridge Mass., 1970.
5 Maynard, A., *op. cit.*
6 Beales, A. F. C., *et al.*, *Education: A Framework for Choice*, Institute of Economic Affairs, 1970.
7 Peston, M., 'Accountability in Education: Some Economic Aspects', *Education Policy Bulletin*, Vol. 8, No. 2, Autumn 1980, pp. 115–126.
8 Maynard, A., *op. cit.*, p. 26.
9 Wiseman, J., 'The Economics of Education' *Scottish Journal of Political Economy*, Vol. 6, No. 1, 1959, pp. 48–58.
10 West, E. G., *Education and the State*, Institute of Economic Affairs, 2nd ed. 1970, p. 219.
11 Woodhall, M., 'Alternatives in the Finance of Education Vouchers' in *The Finance of Education*, Block IV of Economics and Education Policy, Open University, Course ED322, 1977, p. 81.
12 West, E. G., *Economics, Education and the Politician*, Institute of Economic Affairs, 1968, p. 48.
13 *ibid.* p. 30.
14 *ibid.* p. 29.
15 Wagner, L. 'Vouchers – are they the answer for parental choice' *Education*, Vol. 144, No. 24, 13th December 1974, reprinted in *The Finance of Education*, Open University, Course ED322.
16 Blaug, M., *An Introduction to the Economics of Education*, Allen Lane 1970, p. 315.
17 Weiler, D., *et al.*, *A Public School Voucher Demonstration: The First Year at Alum Rock*, Rand, California, 1974. Summarised in Baxter, C., *et al.*, *Economics and Education Policy: a Reader*, Longman, 1977.

18 Cohen, D. K. and Farrar, E., 'Power to the Parents? – the story of education vouchers', *The Public Interest*, No. 48, Summer 1977, pp. 72–97.
19 Barker, P., *et al., A Study in Alternatives in American Education*, Vol. V, *Diversity in the Classroom.*, Rand, California, 1981, p. iv.
20 Cohen and Farrar, *op. cit.*
21 Barker, P., *et al., op. cit.*, p. xii.
22 Cohen and Farrar, *op. cit.*
23 *ibid.*
24 Capell, F. J., *A Study of Alternatives in American Education*, Vol. VI, *Student Outcomes at Alum Rock 1974–76* Rand, Santa Monica, July 1981, pp. viii, ix, 79.
25 This account is largely derived from *Education Vouchers in Kent*, A Feasibility Study for the Education Department of Kent County Council, 1978.
26 *ibid.* p. 39.
27 Levin, H. M., 'Educational Vouchers and Social Policy' in Guthrie, J. W. ed., *School Finance Policies and Practices*, Bellinger, 1980, p. 254.
28 Maynard, A., 'The Finance of Higher Education by a System of Student Loan', evidence to the House of Commons Committee on Education Science and Art, 21st May 1980, House of Commons 5th Report HC 787/11.
29 Crew, M. A. and Young, A., *Paying by Degrees*, Institute of Economic Affairs, 1977.
30 A useful summary can be found in Cohn E., *The Economics of Education*, Ballinger, 2nd Ed. 1979, p. 290f.
31 Mishan, E. J., *Making the World Safe for Pornography and Other Intellectual Fashions*, Alcove Press, 1973, Ch. 1.
32 Peacock, A. T. and Wiseman, J., *Education for Democrats*, Institute of Economic Affairs, 1964, p. 36f.
33 Glennerster H., Merrett, S. and Wilson, G., 'A Graduate Tax' *Higher Education Review*, Vol. 1, No. 1, 1968, pp. 26–36.
34 *ibid.*
35 Maynard, A., *op. cit.*, p. 53.
36 Woodhall, M., 'The Arguments for and against Loans' in Baxter, C., *et al., Economics and Education Policy: a Reader*, Longman, 1977, p. 332.
37 Maynard, A., *op. cit.*, p. 58.
38 Mishan, E. J., quoted in Woodhall *op. cit.*
39 Maynard, A., Memorandum submitted to the Committee on Education Science and Arts, *The Finance of Higher Education by a system of Student Loans*, House of Commons 5th Report, 1980, HC 787/11.
40 Blaug, M., *op. cit.*, p. 298.
41 Maynard, A., *op. cit.*, p. 59.
42 National Union of Students, *Why we don't need loans: some current questions answered.*
43 Committee on Higher Education, *Higher Education: Report of the Committee under the Chairmanship of Lord Robbins*, Cmnd. 2154, HMSO 1963, p. 211.
44 Woodhall, M., *Student Loans: Lessons from Recent International Experience*, Policy Studies Institute, London, 1982.

45 Leonard, K. J., 'Skipping out on Alma Mater: Some Problems Involving the Collection of Federal Student Loans' *Columbia Journal of Law and Social Problems*, Vol. 15, No. 3, 1980, pp. 317–58.
46 Lewis A., Sandford C., Thomson N., *Grants or Loans*, Institute of Economic Affairs, 1980.
47 *Royal Commission on the Distribution of Income and Wealth*, Report, HMSO, 1975, Table 23.
48 Jencks, C., *et al.*, *Inequality*, Harper & Row, 1972.
49 Byrne, D., *et al.*, *The Poverty of Education*, Martin Robertson, 1975, p. 6.
50 Husen, T., quoted in *Education Equity and Income Distribution*, Course ED322, Open University, 1977.
51 Psaracharopoulus, G., 'Family Background, Education and Achievement', *British Journal of Sociology*, September 1977.
52 Quoted in Glennester, H., 'Education and Inequality' in Rubenstein, D., ed., *Education and Equality*, Penguin, 1979.
53 Cohn, E., *Economics of Education*, Balinger, 2nd Ed. 1979, p. 51.
54 Husen, T., *The School in Question*, Oxford University Press, 1979, p. 75.
55 Johns, R. L. and Morphet, E. L., *The Economics and Financing of Education*, Prentice Hall, NJ, 3rd Ed. 1975, p. 100.
56 Thurow, L., 'Education and Economic Equality', *Public Interest* 1972, reprinted in Baxter, C. *et al.* eds, *Economics and Education Policy*, Longman, 1977.
57 Halsey, A. H., 'Social Mobility and Education' in Rubinstein, D., ed., *Education and Equality*, Penguin, 1979.
58 Husen, T., *op. cit.*, p. 90.
59 Vaizey, J. and Sheehan, J., *Resources for Education*, Allen & Unwin, 1968, p. 5.
60 Guthrie, J. W., *et al.*, *Schools and Inequality*, MIT Press, 1971, p. 123.
61 Jordan, K. F. and McKeown, M. P., 'Equity in Financing Public Elementary and Secondary Schools' in *School Finance Policies and Practices*, ed. Guthrie, J. W., Ballinger 1980.
62 Johns, R. L. and Morphet, E. L., *op. cit.* p. 182f.
63 Cohn, E., *op. cit.*, p. 285.
64 Guthrie, J. W., *et al.*, *op. cit.*, p. 129.
65 Byrne, E. M., *Planning and Educational Inequality*, NFER, 1974, p. 304/5.
66 Taylor, G. and Ayres, N., *Born and Bred Unequal*, Longman, 1970, p. 78/79.
67 Tunley, P., Travers, T. and Pratt, J., *Depriving the Deprived*, Kogan Page, 1979, p. 73f.
68 Byrne, D., *op. cit.*, p. 111/112, 157.
69 Pyle, D., 'Resource Allocation in Education', *Social and Economic Administration*, Vol. 10, No. 2, Summer 1976, pp. 106–22.
70 Jallade, J. P., 'Financing Higher Education: the Equity Aspects', *Comparative Education Review*, Vol. 22, No. 2, June 1978, pp. 309–25.
71 Psaracharopoulos, G., 'The Perverse Effects of Public Subsidisation of Education', *Comparative Education Review*, Vol. 21, No. 1, February 1977, pp. 69–89.
72 Drake, K., 'Problem of financing an education system based on the con-

cept of lifelong learning' in Himmelstrup, P., Robinson, J. and Fielden, D. eds, *Strategies for Lifelong Learning*, Esbjerg, 1981, pp. 145–68.

73 McDowell, L., 'Regional inequality and higher education in England and Wales' *Higher Education Review*, Vol. 13, No. 3, Summer 1981, pp. 17–25.

74 West, E. G., *Education and the State*, Institute of Economic Affairs, 2nd Ed. 1970, Ch. 5.

75 Lucas, J. R., 'Equality in Education' in *Education Equality and Society*, ed. Wilson B., Allen & Unwin, 1975.

76 Garms, W. I., Guthrie, J. W. and Pierce, L. C., *School Finance: The Economics and Politics of Public Education*, Prentice Hall, NJ, 1978, p. 22f.

77 Bowman, M. J., 'Education and Opportunity; some Economic Perspectives', *Oxford Review of Education*, Vol. 1, No. 1, 1975, p. 73–84.

78 Neave, G., *Patterns of Equality*, NFER, 1976, p. 62f.

79 Johns, R. L., 'Improving the Equity of School Finance Programs', *Journal of Educational Finance*, Vol. 1, Spring 1976.

80 Halsey, A. H., *op. cit.*

8

Efficiency in Education

Efficiency is concerned with the relationship between inputs and outputs. This may seem obvious, but at times when governments are striving to reduce public expenditure, it is all too easy for them to make the assumption that resources can be cut without this having any effect on output. Whilst this may occur in some cases, it is equally likely that cuts in inputs may lead to proportionately greater falls in what is produced, so that the result of cuts may be that the system becomes less efficient.

In order to consider efficiency it is necessary to differentiate between two kinds of efficiency: technical and economic. Technical efficiency is concerned with the relationship between quantities of inputs and outputs. In a factory producing a specific product, such as chairs, this is relatively easy to analyse: a process of trial and error could establish a suitable relationship between resources, such as the number of workers and machines on the one hand and the quantity of chairs produced on the other. In education the analysis is more difficult, largely because the output is less clear. As Chapter 3 showed, output is so varied that it is difficult or impossible to calculate. However, in specific instances teachers may be able to conclude that a certain approach is technically most efficient. For example if there are twenty five students wishing to take GCE A level Chemistry, it would be possible to organise this in a variety of ways – using one or more teachers and/or laboratory assistants; giving more or fewer lessons to the whole group; varying the size of groups in classes and laboratory. The output in this case – narrowly defined – is the number and grade of A level passes. Careful analysis should make it possible, in theory at least, to reach a technically efficient solution which maximised the relationship between outputs and inputs.

More important than technical efficiency is economic efficiency. This takes account not only of the quantities of resources, but also of their cost. An activity is economically efficient if it achieves a given level of output at the lowest possible cost, or alternatively if it achieves the maximum possible output given the relative prices of the available resources. The difference between technical and economic efficiency can be seen most clearly in examples removed from education. It may be technically efficient to plough fields and gather corn in India using tractors and combine-harvesters, but, since labour is so cheap, that would be economically inefficient, because it would use an expensive resource – capital equipment – when an inexpensive one – labour – is available. It may be technically efficient in the Chemistry class discussed above to use a good deal of teacher time, but this may be economically inefficient, since that is a relatively expensive resource. The difference between the two concepts is that economic efficiency makes use of the notion of opportunity cost – the value of what is given up when an action is undertaken. It is economically inefficient to use teachers to undertake clerical tasks such as duplicating, which could be undertaken by lower paid staff. Similarly, a class of pupils doing nothing – for example, waiting for a teacher – is an expensive resource lying idle.

Cost-Effectiveness

The prime difficulty involved in analysing efficiency in education is the problem of measuring and valuing output. To some extent this difficulty can be minimised by using a cost-effectiveness approach.

Cost-effectiveness studies begin by defining the objectives to be achieved. These may vary from the general (providing primary education to x number of children in a village) to the specific (learning the Highway Code). Then various ways are considered which could be used to achieve these objectives. The costs of these alternatives are then calculated and related to the outcomes. If the objective was to provide adequate primary education to a rural community, various alternative programmes could be adopted:

1 The existing provision could be maintained.
2 A new school could be built, perhaps taking in additional children from surrounding areas.
3 The children could be transferred to nearby schools which have spare capacity.
4 They could be transferred to nearby schools which may then need extending.

Each of these alternatives would have differing cost implications. The objective – providing satisfactory primary education – would be achieved in each case, though the education received would not be identical and there would be differing consequences outside the education system, for example to a village if its school was closed.

The concept of cost-effectiveness differs from that of efficiency. It is possible for a programme to be efficient but not cost effective if the outputs which are actually produced do not contribute to the programme objectives; that is it may be efficient at doing the wrong things. A programme may be effective but neither efficient nor cost-effective if it achieves its goals but wastes resources in doing so.[1]

There are relatively few examples of cost-effectiveness applied to education, but one example of the technique's potential is shown in a study by Thomas. He took as his objective the achievement of GCE A level Economics and examined its provision in four institutions: a school, two sixth form colleges and a college of further education. He made use of two approaches. In the first of these, inputs were calculated with money values, such as teachers' salaries and student earnings foregone, whilst the second approach used weighted GCE O level scores as a measure of input. These two alternative measures of inputs were related to the number and grade of A levels in Economics obtained in each institution. Using the costed approach the best result was obtained by the college of further education; using O levels as an input the best result was obtained by one of the sixth form colleges.[2] It is, of course, not possible to generalise from such a small sample and Thomas's results are of less importance than the method which highlights many of the difficulties involved. Not the least of these is that of obtaining the data.

Input-Output Analysis

A technique of growing interest to economists analysing education is that of input-output analysis. As the phrase suggests, the basic idea is to analyse the extent of the inputs and outputs and consider the relationship between them. The usual way in which this is done is to make use of a production function. This was discussed in the context of the entire economy in Chapter 4, but it can also be used to analyse efficiency in smaller units.

A production function is a mathematical statement of the relationship between various inputs and outputs, arrived at by trial and error and analyses which suggest the best combination of inputs needed to produce the output. In a factory, for example, the inputs may be *x* workers working *y* machines and using *z* quantities of raw materials.

A simplified educational production function may take the following form:

$$O = f \ (A, B, C, D)$$

This suggests that educational output (O) is a function of inputs A, B, C and D, where A represents a variety of measures of the school environment, such as its physical facilities, the amount and quality of teaching, and the amount of time the student is exposed to these influences; B represents a variety of individual and family background characteristics, such as social class and parental income and education; C represents the student's ability and initial level of learning, whilst E represents a variety of peer group influences. The *f* indicates that these inputs combine in a particular way to produce the output; for example it may suggest that output is largely functionally determined by individual and family background with other inputs being less important.

The aim of research in this area is to discover precisely what these inputs are, and what the relationship between them should be, in order to maximise the relationship between input and output. Since some of the inputs, such as family background, cannot be changed, attention is usually concentrated on the variables measuring school environment. In other words – does school make a difference?

The technique is perhaps best illustrated by an example. Cohn and Millman analysed data from fifty three Pennsylvania high schools.[3] They considered twelve outputs which ranged from basic mathematical and verbal skills, to psychological and attitudinal aspects, such as the child's self-concept and interest in school, creativity and health habits. These were generally measured by performance on a series of tests. Their input variables were extensive. Those relating to teachers for example included years in present position, type of college from which graduated, educational level of teacher's mother (!), as well as teacher aspiration, satisfaction, classroom practices, salary, experience, education and teaching load. There were also related variables – staff-student ratio, administrative support and so on. Other inputs included class size, attendance, library facilities, extra-curricular expenditure and administrative support.

All these inputs and outputs were related together in a series of equations. Although the researchers felt that their empirical results were disappointing, they did discover some interesting relationships. Thus output was higher where teachers had a low teaching load and where teachers salaries were higher. More use of para-professionals seemed to be linked to lower output.

There have been a number of similar studies. Bridge *et al.* analysed the results of twenty eight major studies.[4] It is not possible to summarise their results adequately here, but perhaps a flavour may be useful. Thus students with experienced teachers do better than those with less experienced teachers. Students achieve more when the teacher has a more specialised teaching load, and when the teacher has high verbal ability the students also have high achievement in this area.

Other factors which increase student achievement include higher spending per pupil, low teacher turnover, high teacher salaries, satisfactory physical plant, length of school year and kindergarten attendance. The child's achievement and positive self-concept are also linked to increased achievement as are parental education, occupation and income.

Factors which seem to make little or no difference include pupil's housing arrangements, teacher's marital status, school size and age of school building and availability of library books.

These results are included more as a sample of the kind of relationships which can be explored using input-output analysis rather than as universal relationships. In the first place some of the results are found by only one or two researchers, and some relationships are indirect and heavily qualified. In any event it is not clear that relationships which are significant in American high schools will be of any importance in other contexts. One cannot transfer research findings in social science across time and distance.

Even in their own context there are a number of critics of this approach. Levin argues that schools are not technically efficient in producing achievement and that inefficiencies may be substantial.[5] This is because in Levin's view the principal function of schools is not to maximise cognitive achievements but to reproduce the social relations of production, for example by socialising pupils into accepting hierarchical relationships. Moreover, school administrators have very little knowledge of how to improve achievement scores, and the reward structure of schools (such as giving higher salaries) is not used to benefit those teachers whose students obtain high achievement. The significance of this argument is that production function coefficients do not represent what *could* be accomplished, but rather measure what is actually achieved in existing schools which are probably inefficient.

There are other difficulties. On the input side, probably no single input has much effect by itself. It is the interrelationship between inputs which is important and this is difficult if not impossible to ascertain or reproduce in other schools, particularly since so many educational decisions are made by the unobserved teacher in the classroom. Many of the inputs are proxies for the qualities we would like to measure but cannot, for example the 'good teacher', so instead researchers use substitutes for this, such as experience, qualifications or salary. As Hanushek points out, the important dimensions of teacher quality are not captured by measured teacher attributes.[6]

These input difficulties are small, however, compared to those on the other side of the equation. The typical analysis makes use of standardised achievement tests which cannot measure many of the most important qualities which schools would wish their pupils to attain. Schools run by religious bodies may have as their first and paramount goal that of ensuring that students become good Christians. An otherworldly test is needed to measure this!

Any conclusions arising from input-output analysis must be tentative, for education is too complex for simple, universal solutions. Even if clear relationships between inputs and outputs could be discovered, that would not be the whole story, for critics such as Vaizey claim that this approach 'is asking the wrong question; that the improvement in school conditions is an end in itself, rather as when people grow better off they substitute better quality food for poor quality food, and therefore to look at the educational system as an input-output system is an error'.[7]

Class Size

Research into the relationship between class size and pupil achievement illustrates the limitations and problems inherent in analysing the relationship between inputs and output. Since teacher salaries are the largest cost in education it is not surprising that this has been the subject of extensive analysis. As long ago as the seventeenth century Comenius wrote:

> I maintain that it is not only possible for one teacher to teach hundreds of scholars at once, but that it is also essential; since for both the teachers and their pupils it is by far the most advantageous system. The larger the number of pupils he sees before him the greater the interest the teacher will take in his work . . . and the keener the teacher himself, the greater the enthusiasm that his pupils will display.[8]

Since that time there have been hundreds of research studies into the relationship between class size and pupil achievement, covering a wide variety of subjects, skills and age groups. The usual picture given by these researchers has been to suggest that smaller classes do not in general give rise to higher standards. A typical comment was that of Fleming in 1959. After reviewing many studies he concluded:

> there have been many investigations; but with few exceptions, it has had to be reported that, under typical conditions, class size in itself appears to be an unimportant factor. The benefits of small classes, though commonly taken for granted by theorists, are as yet largely undemonstrated in the pages of accredited research reports.[9]

Nearly twenty years later another summary of research concluded:

> the research provides no clearcut guidelines for an 'optimum' class size covering all types of students at all grade levels. . . . There is general concensus that the research findings on the effect of class size on pupil achievement across all grade levels are contradictory and inconclusive. . . . Existing research findings do not support the contention that smaller classes will of themselves result in greater economic achievement gains for pupils.[10]

These research findings contrast strongly with the opinion expressed by most teachers that academic standards do rise when classes are smaller. This belief is supported by one rather unusual kind of review of the literature. Glass and Smith looked at some eighty studies of the relationship between class size and achievement, and from these studies they obtained over seven hundred comparisons between smaller and larger classes. Using regression analysis these were integrated into a single curve which 'revealed a definite inverse relationship between class size and pupil learning. . . . As class size increases achievement decreases. . . . The major benefits from reduced class size are obtained as size is reduced below 20 pupils'. The last sentence of their report concluded: 'there is little doubt that, other things being equal, more is learned in smaller classes'.[11]

There are a number of reasons for the contradictory findings. Glass and Smith were essentially adding together all the previous findings, excluding those researches which they felt were faulty. In that sense their sample was self-selected and may obscure real differences in the quality of the research they included. Their work has also been criticised on statistical grounds.[12]

The relationship between class size and achievement is difficult to research. It is not obvious what is the 'class' and how many students it contains, particularly when there are differing forms of organisation practiced in the school, or when absenteeism varies significantly. Moreover, it is not at all clear what is meant by 'large' or 'small'. There have been studies where 'small' classes were anything under forty and 'large' classes were over fifty. There have been other studies where 'small' classes were defined as having less than fifteen students, whilst 'large' classes were those with over twenty five.[13]

It is also clear that the ideal size of class will vary with the circumstances, particularly the age and the ability of the pupil, the method of teaching and the type of achievement that is aimed for. In learning to drive a car a class of one is ideal, whilst a group of a hundred might be quite satisfactory for a lecture in higher education or for a film.

There are less obvious difficulties. The majority of investigations have been handicapped by an undue concentration on a very narrow band of educational outcomes, such as can be easily measured by externally normed achievement tests.[14] The most important educational outcomes are often precisely those which are difficult to measure by tests. These include not only pupil attitudes, interaction and socialisation, but also the higher level academic skills, such as analysis and application. These may be the precise outcomes which are stimulated in small group situations.

The position is also complicated by teacher attitudes and styles of teaching. Teachers with small classes may use styles of teaching more suited to large group situations. The economist would also add that other inputs besides labour may be changing at the same time. In an ideal world what would be needed would be experiments in which the interrelationships between inputs and outputs were explored in a variety of controlled situations. Since that is unlikely, the possibilities arising from class size research seem limited. The ideal class size – if there is such a thing – will vary with the circumstances. The question to be asked is 'what combination of resources and techniques would be efficient in this particular situation?' Research on class size shows little sign of answering that question.

Size of School

If the size of classes is a matter for controversy, so is the size of schools. Are big schools better or is small beautiful? To pose questions such as this is really to ask what is the relationship between inputs and outputs at varying sizes of schools.

So far as costs are concerned, there is some reason to believe that within limits, schools, like firms, may give rise to economies of scale. By this phrase economists mean that as size increases, average cost falls. These economies may arise in a number of ways. Building costs may be relatively lower in large schools, because communal facilities such as halls or libraries are needed even in small schools. Similarly, expensive facilities such as pianos or computers may be cheaper per pupil in large schools, because their cost can be spread out over many pupils.

However the largest cost is that of staff, and here the position is rather more complex. The marginal cost of an additional pupil in a class or school is very low because no extra staff are required. If a policy is adopted whereby no primary class exceeds thirty pupils then a school with an entry of sixty one pupils will need three teachers per year group; so will a school with ninety entrants. Clearly the larger schools will be much less expensive on a per pupil basis. This is one reason why it is often much less expensive to close small schools and to transport children to nearby schools where there are vacancies.

In secondary schools the position is more complex, because it is not just teachers that are required, but teachers with particular specialisms. Even a small secondary school will need male and female PE teachers, language teachers and so on, though the number of specialised staff required is also influenced by the curriculum, in particular by how many options are provided. This is particularly important in the sixth form, where class sizes are usually smaller than in the rest of the school. Webb analysed the number of staff required in various sizes of sixth form. Making various assumptions, such as that groups could vary between five and eighteen pupils for A level classes, he calculated that ten teachers would be required when the number of sixth formers was between fifty and a hundred or so. At some point more teachers would be required to duplicate groups, so that if more than a hundred and ten pupils enrolled the number of teachers required would rise to thirteen. This number can cope until the number of students rises to two hundred when seventeen teachers are needed. In this kind of model it is clear that average cost per pupil is considerably lower in large sixth forms. Note however that the fall in costs is not smooth, but in steps as shown in Table 8.1.[15]

There have been a number of studies relating cost to size. Katzman reviewed American research and concluded that optimum enrolment for high schools was around 2000 pupils or 80 teachers, though there was a good deal of variation between studies.[16] These results may not be transferrable to other countries where the whole organisation of the school is different. A more recent analysis by Smith concluded:

> Firstly, generally speaking, economies of scale, expressed in terms of reducing per pupil expenditure, can be observed up to a certain level when significant economies may be reduced. Secondly, the process of schooling itself – the internal organisation of the school – is shown to be an important factor in the achievement of any economies.[17]

In other words, average cost falls as size of school increases, but this process does not continue *ad infinitum*. At some point, depending on how the school is organised, there will be no cost advantages to be obtained by increasing size. Hough's researches suggest that in English secondary schools minimum average cost ceases to fall once schools have reached between 980 and 1200 pupils.[18]

So far this analysis of school size has been concerned with costs, or in other words, with inputs. However there have been many suggestions that the quality of education will be effected by the size of school, though this seems to have little effect on academic achievement, since other factors, such as pupil characteristics or teacher ability, are probably more important. Typical findings are those of Burkhead who found that size did not affect reading achievements of high school pupils[19] and Sabulao and Hickrod who obtained similar results in mathematics.[20] Pupils in very small schools may have lower achievement because there are fewer facilities, but analysis is difficult because size of school is also

Table 8.1 *Staff Requirements and Costs for Sixth Forms*

	A	*B*	*C*	*D*	*E*
No. of pupils	65	104	156	208	260
No. of staff	10	10	13.2	16.7	16.7
Total teaching cost	£60 000	£60 000	£97 000	£101 000	£101 000
Average teacher cost/per pupil	£908	£577	£512	£486	£389

Source: Webb, P. C., 'Teaching Cost Models for Sixth Forms', *Educational Policy Bulletin*, No. 7, Vol. 1, Spring 1979, Table 4.

associated with other variables, such as urban or rural location which may also affect achievement.[21] The most comprehensive analysis was that of Husen who looked at mathematics achievement in ten countries at age thirteen and in the final year of school. Among thirteen-year-old pupils those in the largest schools obtained the highest scores. In comprehensive schools those in the final year of school did best in the largest schools, though in selective schools scores were higher where there were between 700–1100 pupils, rather than in bigger schools. There were significant national variations from this pattern; for example in Scotland thirteen-year-olds in comprehensives did best in small schools.[22]

Proponents of large schools argue that achievement tests do not tell the whole story. Research confirms that large schools can offer more subject choice, more teacher specialisation and also a wider variety of activities.[23] However, the same researchers suggest that pupils in small schools are more likely to participate in such activities and to gain more satisfactions.

Those who like small schools claim that large size leads to inter-department rivalries,[24] greater staff time spent on meetings and administrative problems[25] and that 'with increasingly impersonal patterns of control, personal contact with the Headmaster and personal knowledge by him of all activities within the school, which seems in the English system, at least, to have been some measure of quality, is progressively lost'.[26]

The supporters of large schools believe that the disadvantages can be overcome, and that prejudice rather than fact or analysis is often the main factor motivating their critics. A report by the Secondary Heads Association claimed that: 'the evidence on school size however, is consistent and clear. While less tangible aspects of school life my well be of importance, these are independent of school size, which does not matter in itself' and a few pages later they conclude, with perhaps some inconsistency: 'One is left with the inevitable conclusion that, in practice as well as in theory, big *is* beautiful'.[27]

Efficiency and Educational Technology

It is rather surprising that the education industry, which has undergone so many curriculum changes, should show so few signs of technical innovation. It seems appropriate therefore to ask whether the costs of introducing technology are so great compared to the benefits, that such innovation is not worthwhile? Or does the reason lie with individual or institutional constraints on innovation?

Rather like economics, educational technology can be defined by its objective matter, or by its intellectual method.[28] As with economics, it is easier to perceive the matter – TV, films, computers and so on – rather than the method, a systematic approach to instruction.

The use of educational technology promises higher output and/or lower costs. Greater learning may occur because different, more suitable methods can be used. The methods will vary with the medium, but several of the media such as computer-based learning, allow individualised instruction where students can learn at their own pace. Moreover, if alternative learning methods are available, students can choose that which they find most appropriate. Some of the media may be particularly appropriate to some types of learning.

Another advantage is that the materials may be better prepared than an individual teacher could manage, and they may be carried to a wider audience. The best example of this is the Open University, where the course units are prepared with a care that no individual lecturer could offer. Once prepared, the materials can be used in a wide variety of locations, including other institutions of higher education.

In school situations materials are often used as an extra help to teachers rather than a replacement; hence the phrase audio-visual aids. One reason for this is that teachers are needed to maintain control. In the school situation therefore, educational technology tends to increase costs in the expectation of improving learning. In higher education the position is rather different, because the necessity for control disappears and the possibility arises of substituting technology for people; in other words of cutting costs.

Because there are many different types of media, almost any generalisation about their use will have exceptions. However, in general the pattern of costs will vary considerably from those found in 'conventional' teaching. A fundamental difference is that a media based approach demands a far greater investment of resources before any output is obtained.[29] This is particularly true for computer and distance learning, where the fixed costs are usually very large. This means that the scale of the operation is important. If fixed costs are large, the approach will only be economical if these can be spread over many students. That is why an organisation such as the Open University has low costs per student for its foundation courses which are taken by thousands of students each year, but relatively high costs for more specialised courses with only a few hundred students.

The problem of scale is less important when the fixed costs are low. This will often be the case for approaches using media such as overhead projectors, tape recorders or slides, though even here the fixed costs may be greater than is generally realised since an important cost of any innovation is that of the innovator's time. A teacher producing a tape-slide programme must spend many hours in preparation to produce one hour of usable material. That is one reason why educational innovation has proceeded so slowly.

One of the difficulties involved in assessing the efficiency of educational technology is that it is not always easy to identify which costs are involved. A good example of this would be an innovation where staff work part-time on a project, but spend the rest of their time on other activities such as teaching. This also applies to support staff, such as secretaries and technicians, whose time is often spent on a variety of courses. Another important question is – who pays the cost? On many projects, much student time is involved in the testing and development stages, but this is frequently ignored when costs are being analysed, because those initiating the project do not have to pay students.

Whether an innovation is efficient, however, does not depend on total costs, important though those are. What is important are the costs per user. An expensive innovation may be efficient if it is used extensively. In planning it is therefore necessary to estimate utilisation rates and in some cases this is relatively easy. A particular institution may be able to forecast student use fairly accurately for internal students, but for systems which have to be purchased or used by outsiders, the forecasting is less easy and hugh errors may occur. Wagner gives as an example of the magnitude of error which may occur the estimates produced for PLATO IV, a large scale computer assisted instruction system centred on the University of Illinois. In 1970 estimates suggested a maximum cost of $0.68 per student contact hour. In 1973 the actual average cost per contact hour was just under $7.[30] The reason was largely that student utilisation was much less than forecast.

Although evidence is available on the costs of using different media,[35] it is not easy to generalise from the data, for example to define the circumstances under which a particular innovation, such as computer assisted learning, would be efficient. One reason for this is that the media themselves are constantly changing, but a more important factor is that an innovation designed for one situation may yield different results and have different costs if applied in a different location and under different circumstances.

Whilst high labour costs offer incentives to innovate through the use of educational technology, the evidence so far suggests that the incentives have had relatively little effect. One reason is that an incentive which is successful in one place may be ignored in another. The diffusion of innovation is very slow in education. This may be because staff lack adequate training, or because teachers feel that their autonomy is threatened by new techniques which require them to adapt to new ways of teaching and which may require more preparation. The geographical and administrative structure of the school may also inhibit the use of new methods. Equipment locked away at the other end of the school may be too much trouble to use. School store rooms are full of equipment gathering dust, untouched except at stocktaking. Other staff may have to agree to changes and new methods may not fit conveniently into timetabled peiods. Change involves difficulties and it is easier to continue with the old ways. In education the innovator may receive few rewards.

Conclusion

After reviewing all the evidence, one is left to conclude that any statement about efficiency in education must be extremely tentative, largely because the problem of measuring output presents such difficulties. So far as costs are concerned, it is clear that very small classes and schools are expensive and that there may be a strong economic case for amalgamations and closures. The price to be paid for these, however, is less easily measured, for the teachers and pupils involved may experience substantial upheaval.

The great danger in studying efficiency in education is that simplistic conclusions will be reached; to say, in effect, that, since measuring output is difficult, whatever is cheapest is best. Such conclusions must be resisted. At its best, education is life enhancing, and an inability to measure this is no reason to ignore it.

References

1 Simkins, T., *Economics and the Management of Resources*, Sheffield Papers in Education Management, Sheffield Polytechnic, 1981, p. 80.
2 Thomas, H. R., 'Cost-effectiveness Analysis as a Method of Assessing "A" Level Performance in Different Educational Establishments', *Educational Studies*, Vol. 7, No. 2, 1981, pp. 95–103.
3 Cohn, E. and Millman, S. D., *Input-Output Analysis in Public Education*, Ballinger, 1975.
4 Bridge, R. G., Judd, C. M. and Moock, P. R., *The Determinants of Educational Outcomes*, Ballinger, 1979.
5 Levin, H. M., 'Concepts of Economic Efficiency and Educational Production' in *Education as an Industry*, eds Froomkin, J. T., Jamison, D. T. and Radner, R., Ballinger, 1976, p. 13.
6 Hanushek, E. A., 'Conceptual and Empirical Issues in the Estimation of Education Production Functions', *Journal of Human Resources*, Vol. XIV, No. 3, Summer 1979, pp. 351–87.
7 Vaizey, J., 'The School in Question: an economists viewpoint', *Oxford Review of Education*, Vol. 5, No. 3, October 1979, pp. 207–14.
8 Comenius, quoted in Fleming, C. M., 'Class Size as a Variable in the Teaching Situation', *Educational Research*, Vol. 1, No. 2, 1959, pp. 35–48.
9 Fleming, C. M., *op. cit.*
10 Educational Research Services Inc., *Class Size: A Summary of Research*, USA, 1978.

11 Glass, G. V. and Smith, M. L., *Meta-Analysis of Research on the Relationship of Class Size and Achievement*, Laboratory of Educational Research, University of Colorado, 1970.
12 Cullen, B. D., 'Lessons from Class Size Research – an economist's perspective', *Trends in Education*, Winter 1979, pp. 29–33.
13 Ross, D. H. and McKenna, B., *Class Size: The Multi Dollar Question*, Teachers College, Columbia University, NY, 1955.
14 Burstall, C., 'Time to mend the nets: a commentary on the outcomes of class size research', *Trends in Education*, Autumn 1979, pp. 27–33.
15 Webb, P. C., 'Teaching Cost Models for Sixth Forms', *Educational Policy Bulletin*, Vol. 7, No. 1, Spring 1979, pp. 43–65.
16 Katzman, M. T., *The Political Economy of Urban Schools*, Harvard University Press, 1971, p. 89.
17 Smith, R., 'Comprehensive Schools: the Problem of Appropriate Size', in *A Volume of Essays for Elizabeth Halsall*, eds Brock, C. and Ryba, R. University of Hull Institute of Education, 1980, p. 30.
18 Hough, J. R., *A Study of School Costs*, NFER, 1981.
19 Burkhead, J., *Input and Output in Large City High Schools*, Syracuse University Press, NY, 1967.
20 Sabulao, C. M. and Hickrod, G. A., 'Optimum Size of School Districts relative to selected costs', *Journal of Educational Administration*, Vol. IX, No. 2, October 1971, pp. 178–92.
21 Ross, J. M., *et al.*, *A Critical Appraisal of Comprehensive Education*, NFER, 1972, p. 174.
22 Husen, T., ed., *International Study of Achievement in Mathematics*, Vol. II, Wiley, 1967.
23 *See* Barker, R. G. and Gump, P. V., *Big School, Small School: High School Size and Student Behaviour*, Stanford University Press, 1964, and Campbell, W. J., 'School Size: its influence on Pupils', *Journal of Educational Administration*, Vol. 3, No, 1, May 1965, pp. 3–17, Ross, J. M., *op. cit.*
24 Musgrove, F., 'Curriculum Objectives', *Journal of Curriculum Studies*, Vol. 1, No. 1, 1968, pp. 5–18.
25 Taylor, W., *Heading for Change*, HTV Publications, Cardiff 1969.
26 Smith, R., *op. cit.*
27 Secondary Heads Association, *Big and Beautiful*, 1979.
28 Layard, R. and Oatey, M., 'Cost Effectiveness of the New Media in Higher Education', in Lumsden, K., ed., *Efficiency in Universities: the La Paz Papers*, Elsevier, 1974.
29 Wagner, L., *The Economics of Educational Media*, Macmillan, 1982, p. 84.
30 *ibid.* p. 86,
31 Jamison, D., Klees, S. and Wells, S. J., *Cost Analysis for Educational Planning and Evaluation*, Agency for International Development, USA, 1976.

Bibliography

Alexander, K., 'The Value of an Education', *Journal of Educational Finance* Vol. 1, No. 4, Spring 1976, pp. 429–67.

Alt, J. E., 'Some Social and Political Correlates of County Borough Expenditure', *B.J. Political Science*, Vol. 1 Pt 1, 1971.

Ashenfelter, O. and Ham, J., 'Education, Unemployment and Earnings', *Journal of Political Economy*, Vol. 87, No. 5, Pt 2, 1979, pp. S99–S115.

Atkinson, G. B. J., 'The Value of a B Ed Degree', *Higher Education Review*, Vol. 7, No. 3, Summer 1975, pp. 60–63.

Austen, Jane, *Emma*, Collins, 1952 ed.

Balogh, T. and Streeten, P. P., 'The Planning of Education in Poor Countries', in Blaug, M., ed., *Economics of Education 1*, Penguin, 1968.

Barker, P., *et al.*, *A Study in Alternatives in America Education, Vol. V Diversity in the Classroom*, Rand, Calif., 1981.

Barker, R. G. and Gump, P. V., *Big School, Small School: High School Size and Student Behaviour*, Stanford University Press, 1964.

Baumol, W. J., 'On the Social Rate of Discount', *American Economic Review*, Vol. LVIII, December 1968, pp. 788–802.

Baxter, C., O'Leary, P. J. and Westoby, A., *Economics and Education Policy: a reader*, Longman, 1977.

Beales, A. F. C., *et al.*, *Education: A Framework for Choice*, Institute of Economic Affairs, 1970.

Becker, G. S., *Human Capital: A Theoretical and Empirical Analysis*, Princeton University Press, 1964.

Berg, I., *Education and Jobs: the Great Training Robbery*, Beacon Press, 1971.

Birch, D. W. and Calvert, J. R., 'How Profitable is Teaching', *Higher Education Review*, Vol. 6, No. 1, Autumn 1972, pp. 35–44.

Blaug, M., ed., *Economics of Education 1*, Penguin, 1969.

Blaug, M., ed., *Economics of Education 2*, Penguin, 1969.

Blaug, M., *An Introduction to the Economics of Education*, Allen Lane, (Penguin Press), 1970.

Blaug, M., *Education and the Employment Problem in Developing Countries*, International Labour Office, 1973.

Blaug M., 'The Empirical Status of Human Capital Theory: A Slightly Jaundised Survey', *Journal of Economic literature*, Vol. XIV, No. 3, September 1976, pp. 827–55.

Boaden, N., *Urban Policy Making: Influences on County Boroughs in England and Wales*, Cambridge University Press, 1971, Ch. 5.

Bowles, S., 'Schooling and Equality from Generation to Generation', *Journal of Political Economy*, Vol. 80, May/June, pp. 219–51.

Bowles, S. and Gintis, H., 'Economic Analysis of Lifelong Education' in Dave R. H., ed., *Foundations of Lifelong Education*, Pergamon Press for UNESCO, 1976.

Bowman, M. J., 'The Costing of Human Resource Development' in Robinson, E. A. G. and Vaizey, J., eds, *Economics of Education*, Macmillan, 1966.

Bowman, M. J., Anderson, C. A., 'Concerning the role of education in development', in Bowman, M. J., *et al.* eds, *Readings in the Economics of Education*, UNESCO, 1968.

Bowman, M. J., *et al.* eds, *Readings in the Economics of Education*, UNESCO, 1968.

Bowman, M. J., 'Perspectives on Education and Development', in Wykstra, R. A., *Human Capital Formation and Manpower Development*, Free Press, 1971.

Bowman, M. J., 'Education and Opportunity: some Economic Perspectives', *Oxford Review of Education*, Vol. 1, No. 1, 1975, pp. 73–84.

Bramley, G. and Evans, A., 'GREat complexity causes controversy', *Municipal Journal*, 6 February 1981.

Bridge, R. G., Judd, C. M. and Moock, P. R., *The Determinants of Educational Outcomes*, Ballinger, 1979.

Brock, C. and Ryba, R., eds, *A Volume of Essays for Elizabeth Halsall*, University of Hull Institute of Education, 1980.

Burkhead, J., *Input and Output in Large City High Schools*, Syracuse University Press, NY, 1967.

Burstall, C., 'Time to mend the nets: a commentary on the outcomes of class size research', *Trends in Education*, Autumn 1979, pp. 27–33.

Byrne, D., Williamson, B. and Fletcher, B., *The Poverty of Education*, Martin Robertson, 1975.

Byrne, E. M., *Planning and Educational Inequality*, NFER, 1974.

Campbell, W. J., 'School Size: its influence on Pupils', *Journal of Educational Administration*, Vol. 3, No. 1, May 1965, pp. 3–17.

Capell, F. J., A Study of Alternatives in America, Vol. vi, *Student Outcomes at Alum Rock*, Rand, Santa Monica, California.

Carnoy, M. and Levin, H. M., *The Limits of Educational Reform*, David McKay, 1976, p. 11.

Carter, C., Ermisch, J., Ruffet, F., *Swings for the Schools*, Policy Studies Institute, Vol. XLV, No. 584, December 1979.

Central Statistical Office, *Standard Industrial Classification*, HMSO, 1980.

Chartered Institute of Public Finance and Accountancy, *Education Estimates*, CIPFA, 1983.

Clegg, Standing Commission on Pay Comparability, Report No. 7, *Teachers*, Cmnd 7880, HMSO, 1980.

Cochrane, S. H., *Fertility and Education*, Johns Hopkins University Press, 1979.

Cohen, D. K. and Farrar, E., 'Power to the Parents? – the story of education vouchers', *The Public Interest*, No. 48, Summer 1977, pp. 72–97.

Cohn, E., and Millman, S. D., *Input–Output Analysis in Public Education*, Ballinger, 1975.

Cohn, E., *The Economics of Education*, Ballinger, 2nd Ed. 1979.

Coombs, P. H. and Hallak, J., *Managing Educational Costs*, Oxford University Press, 1972.

Correa, H., 'Sources of Economic Growth in Latin America', *Southern Economic Journal*, No. 37, July 1970, pp. 17–31.

Crew, M. A. and Young, A., *Paying by Degrees*, Institute of Economic Affairs, 1977.

Crispin, A., 'Education and the Rate Support Grant, the case for a Block Education Grant', *Education Policy Bulletin*, Vol. 8, No. 1, Spring 1980, pp. 1–19.

Crispin, A., 'The new Block Grant and Education – Central Control or National Direction?', *Local Government Studies*, November/December 1980, pp. 25–37.

Crowther-Hunt, Lord, 'The Inadequacies of departmental planning in action', *Times Educational Supplement*, 14 May 1976.

Cullen, B. D., 'Lessons from Class Size Research – an economists perspective', *Trends in Education*, Winter 1979, pp. 29–33.

Cumming, C. E., *Studies in Education Cost*, Scottish Academic Press, 1971.

Dave, R. H., ed., *Foundations of Lifelong Education*, Pergamon for UNESCO, 1976.

David, M. E., *Reform, Reaction and Resources: The 3 Rs of Educational Planning*, NFER, 1977.

Davie, R., Butler, N., Goldstein, H., *From Birth to Seven*, Longman, 1972.

Davies, B. P., *Social Needs and Resources in Social Services*, Michael Joseph, 1968.

Dawson, D. A., Determinants of Local Government Expenditure, Appendix 7 of the *Report of the Committee of Enquiry into Local Government Finance* (the Layfield Report), HMSO, 1977.

Denison, E. F., *Accounting for United States Economic Growth 1929–1969*, Brookings Institution, 1974.

Denison, E. F., *Accounting for Slower Economic Growth: The United States in the 1970s*, Brookings Institute, 1979.

Dennison, W. F., 'Expenditure Planning in English Education: Recent developments in the relationship between Central and Local Authorities', *Journal of Educational Administration and History*, Vol. XI, No. 1, January 1979, pp. 34–42.

Dennison, W. F., 'Expenditure Decision Making by English Local Education Authorities', *Education Studies*, Vol. 5, No. 3, October 1979, pp. 241–50.

DES, *The Demand for and Supply of Teachers 1963–86*, Ninth Report of the National Advisory Council on the Training and the Supply of Teachers, HMSO, 1965.

DES, *Student Numbers in Higher Education in England & Wales*, Education Planning Paper, No. 2, HMSO, 1970.

DES, Report on Education, No. 78, *Teacher Turnover*, July, 1973.

DES, Model for Universities Recurrent Grant. Minutes of evidence to the Fifth Report of the Education Science and Arts Committee, *The Funding and Organisation of Courses in H.E.*, Vol. 2, H of C 787 – II, 1980.

DES, *The School Curriculum*, HMSO, 1981.

DES, *Statistics of Education 1979*, Vol. 4, *Teachers*, HMSO, 1981.

DES, 'Secondary School Library Service', *Statistical Bulletin*, 8/81, May, 1981.

DES, *Statistical Bulletin*, 'Teachers in Service', 14/81, 1981.

DES, 'School Statistics: Statistics of Education 1979', *Statistical Bulletin*, 17/81, November 1981.

DES, Statistical Bulletin, 2/82, *Pupil-Teacher Ratios in LEAs in England*, January 1982.

DES, *Statistics of Education 1979*, Vol. 5, *Finance*, HMSO, 1982.

DES, *Report on Education*, 'Trends in School Population', No. 96, November 1979.

Diamond Reports, *Royal Commission on the Distribution of Income and Wealth*, HMSO, 1975.

Drake, K., 'The Importance of Costing Adult Education', *Studies in Adult Education*, Vol. 4, No. 2, October 1972.

Drake, K., *The Cost Effectiveness of Vocational Training: A Survey of British Studies*, mimeograph Manchester University, 1979.

Drake, K., 'Problems of financing an education system based on the concept of lifelong learning', in Himmelstrup, P., Robinson, J. and Fielden, D., eds, *Strategies for Lifelong Learning*, Esbjerg, 1981.

Duncan, G. J., 'Earnings Functions and Non-Pecuniary Benefits', *Journal of Human Resources*, Vol. xi, No. 4, Fall 1976, pp. 462–83.

Durkheim, E., *Education and Sociology*, trans. S. O. Fox, Free Press, 1956.

Educational Research Services Inc, *Class Size: A Summary of Research* USA, 1978.

Edwards, E. O. and Todara, M. P., 'Education and Employment in Developing Countries', in Ward, F. C., ed., *Education and Development Reconsidered*, Praeger, 1974.

Ehrlich, I., 'On the relationship between Education and Crime' in Juster, F. T., ed., *Education Income and Human Behaviour*, McGraw-Hill, 1975.

Else, P. K. and Marshall, G. P., *The Management of Public Expenditure*, Policy Studies Institute, Vol. XLV, No. 580, 1979.

Fagerlind, Ingmar, *Formal Education and Adult Earnings*, Almquist & Wicksell, Stockholm, 1975.

Feldstein, M. S., 'The Social Time Preference Discount Rate', *Economic Journal*, Vol. LXXIV, June 1964, pp. 360–79.

Fleming, C. M., 'Class Size as a Variable in the Teaching Situation', *Educational Research*, Vol. 1, No. 2, 1959, pp. 35–48.

Foster, C. D., Jackman, R., Perlman, M., *Local Government Finance in a Unitary State*, Allen & Unwin, 1980.

Foster, P., 'The Vocation School Fallacy in Development Planning' in Blaug, M., ed., *Economics of Education 1*, Penguin, 1968.

Friedman, M., *Capitalism and Freedom*, University of Chicago Press, 1962.

Froomkin, J. T., Jamison, D. T. and Radner, R., eds, *Education as an Industry*, Ballinger, 1976.

Fulton, O., Gordon, A. and Williams, G., 'Higher Education and Manpower Planning: A Comparison of Planned and Market Economies', *Education Policy Bulletin*, Vol. 8, No. 1, Spring 1980, pp. 83–113.

Garms, W. I., Guthrie, J. W., and Pierce, L. C., *School Finance: The Economics and Politics of Public Education*, Prentice Hall, NJ, 1978.

Glass, G. V., and Smith, M. L., *Meta-Analysis of Research on the Relationship of Class Size and Achievement*, Laboratory of Education Research, University of Colorado, 1970.

Glennerster, H., Merrett, S. and Wilson, G., 'A Graduate Tax', *Higher Education Review*, Vol. 1, No. 1, 1968, pp. 26–36.

Glennerster, H., 'Education and Inequality' in Rubenstein, D., ed., '*Education and Equality*', Penguin, 1979.

Goodman, J. D., 'The Economic Returns to Education: An Assessment of Alternative Models', *Social Science Quarterly*, Vol. 6, No. 2, 1979, pp. 269–83.

Guthrie, J. W., *et al.*, *Schools and Inequality*, MIT Press, 1971.

Guthrie, J. W., ed., *School Finance Policies and Practices*, Ballinger, 1980.

Haddad, W. D., 'The World Bank' – Education Sector Policy Paper: a summary', *Comparative Education*, Vol. 17, No. 2, June 1981, 127–39.

Halsey, A. H., 'Social Mobility and Education' in Rubenstein, D., *Education and Equality*, Penguin, 1979.

Harbison, F. H., *Human Resources as the Wealth of Nations*, Oxford, 1973.

Heclo, H. and Wildavsky, A., *The Private Government of Public Money*, Macmillan, 2nd Ed. 1981.

Heiser, T., 'RSG: Block Grant' in *Public Finance and Accountancy*, March 1981, pp. 13–15.

Henderson-Stewart, D., 'Appendix: Estimates of the Rate of Return to Education in Great Britain', *Manchester School*, Vol. 33, No. 3, 1965, pp. 252–61.

Henry, N. B., ed., *Social Forces Influencing American Education*, University of Chicago Press, 1961.

Hepworth, N. P., *The Finance of Local Government*, Allen & Unwin, 6th Ed. 1980.

Hanushek, E. A., 'Conceptual and Empirical Issues in the Estimation of Education Production Functions', *Journal of Human Resources*, Vol. XIV, No. 3, Summer 1979, pp. 351–87.

Hicks, N. L., 'Growth v Basic Needs: Is there a Trade Off?', *World Development*, Vol. 7, 1979, pp. 985–94.

Himmelstrup, P., Robinson, J. and Fielden, D., eds, *Strategies for Lifelong Learning*, Esbjerg, 1981.

Hinchcliffe, K., 'Teachers, the Open University and the Rates of Return', *Higher Education Review*, Vol. 3, No. 3, Summer 1971, pp. 49–55.

HMSO, *Alternatives to Domestic Rates*, Cmnd 8449, HMSO, 1981.

Hough, J. R., *A Study of School Costs*, NFER, 1981.

House of Commons, *5th Report on the Funding and Organisation of Courses in Higher Education*, Vol. 2, HC 787/2, June 1980.

Howick, C. and Hassani, H., 'Education Spending: Primary' in the *Centre for Environmental Studies Review*, Vol. 5, 1979, pp. 41–46 and 'Secondary' Vol. 8, 1980, pp. 25–30.

Husen, T., ed., *International Study of Achievement in Mathematics*, Vol. II, Wiley, 1967.

Husen, T., *The School in Question*, Oxford University Press, 1979.

Illich, I., *De schooling Society*, Caldar & Boyars, 1971.

International Labour Office, *Teachers Pay*, Geneva, 1978.

Jallade, J. P., 'Financing Higher Education: the Equity Aspects' *Comparative Education Review*, Vol. 22, No. 2, June 1978, pp. 309–25.

Jamison, D., Klees, S. and Wells, S. J., *Cost Analysis for Educational Planning and Valuation*, Agency for International Development, USA, 1976.

Jencks, C., *et al.*, *Education Vouchers: A Report on Financing Elementary Education by Grants to Parents*, Centre for the Study of Public Policy, Cambridge Mass., 1970.

Jencks, C., *et al.*, *Inequality*, Harper & Row, 1972.

Johns, R. L., 'Improving the Equity of School Finance Programs', *Journal of Educational Finance*, Vol. 1, Spring 1976.

Johns, R. L. and Morphet, E. L., *The Economics and Financing of Education*, Prentice Hall, NJ, 3rd Ed. 1975.

Jones, G. W., 'How to save Local Government' in *Town Hall Power or Whitehall Pawn?*, Institute of Economics Affairs, 1980.

Jordan, K. F. and McKeown, M. P., 'Equity in Financing Public Elementary and Secondary Schools', in *School Finance Policies and Practices*, ed. Guthrie, J. W., Ballinger, 1980.

Juster, F. T., ed., *Education, Income and Human Behaviour*, McGraw-Hill, 1975.

Katzman, M. T., *The Political Economy of Urban Schools*, Harvard University Press, 1971.

Kent County Council Education Department, *Education Vouchers in Kent*, Maidstone, 1978.

Keynes, J. M., *General Theory of Employment Interest and Money*, Macmillan, 1936.

King, D. N., 'Local Government Finance and Autonomy', in *Town Hall Power or Whitehall Pawn?*, Institute of Economic Affairs.

Layard, R., 'Cost Effectiveness of the New Media in Higher Education' in Lumsden, K., ed., *Efficiency in Universities: the La Paz Papers*, Elsevier, 1974.

Layard, P. R. G., Sargan, J. D., Ager, M. E. and Jones, D. J., *Qualified Manpower and Economic Performance*, Allen Lane, 1971.

Layfield Committee, *Report of the Committee of Inquiry into Local Government Finance*, Cmnd 6453, HMSO, 1976.

Lefcowitz, M. J., 'Poverty and Health: A Re-examination', *Inquiry*, March 1973, pp. 3–13.

Lee Kiong-Hock and Pscharapoulos, G., 'International Comparisons of Educational and Economic Indicators Revisited', *World Development*, Vol. 7, 1979, pp. 995–1004.

Leibowitz, A., 'Education and the Allocation of Women's Time' in Juster, F. J., ed., *Education Income and Human Behaviour*, McGraw-Hill, 1975.

Leonard, K. J., 'Skipping out on Alma Mater: Some Problems Involving the Collection of Federal Student Loans', *Columbia Journal of Law and Social Problems*, Vol. 15, No. 3, 1980, pp. 317–58.

Levin, H. M., 'Concepts of Economic Efficiency and Educational Production' in *Education as an Industry*, eds Froomkin, J. T., Jamison, D. T. and Radner, R., Ballinger, 1976.

Levin, H. M., 'Educational Vouchers and Social Policy' in Guthrie, J. W., ed., *School Finance Policies and Practices*, Ballinger, 1980, p. 254.

Lewis, A., Sandford C. and Thomson, H., *Grants or Loans*, Institute of Economic Affairs, 1980.

Lewis, W. A., *The Theory of Economic Growth*, George Allen & Unwin, 1955.

Lomax, D. E., 'A Review of British Research in Teacher Education', *Review of Educational Research*, Vol. 42, No. 3, 1972, pp. 289–326.

Lucas, J. R., 'Equality in Education', in *Education Equality and Society*, ed. Wilson, B., Allen & Unwin, 1975.

Lumsden, K., ed., *Efficiency in Universities: the La Paz Papers*, Elsevier, 1974.

Machlup, F., *Education and Economic Growth*, University of Nebraska Press, 1970.

Maynard, A., *Experiment with Choice in Education*, Institute of Economic Affairs, 1975.

Maynard, A., 'The Finance of Higher Education by a System of Student Loans', Evidence to the *House of Commons Committee on Education Science and Art*, 21st May 1980, House of Commons 5th Report, HC 787/11.

McDowell, L., 'Regional Inequality and Higher Education in England and Wales', *Higher Education Review*, Vol. 13, No. 3, Summer 1981, pp. 17–25.

Mincer, J., 'On the Job Training: Costs, Returns and Some Implications', *Journal of Political Economy*, Vol. LXX, Pt 2, October 1962, pp. 50–79.

Mishan, E. J., *The Costs of Economic Growth*, Penguin, 1969.

Mishan, E. J., *Making the World Safe for Pornography and Other Intellectual Fashions*, Alcove Press, 1973.

Moreh, J., 'Human Capital and Economic Growth: United Kingdom 1951–61', *Economic and Social Review*, September 1971, pp. 73–93.

Morris, V. and Ziderman, A., 'The Economic Return on Investment in Higher Education in England and Wales', *Economic Trends*, No. 211, May 1971, pp. xx–xxxi.

Musgrove, F., 'Curriculum Objectives', *Journal of Curriculum Studies*, Vol. 1, No. 1, 1968, pp. 5–18.

National Union of Students, *Why we don't need loans: some current questions answered*, NUS, London.

Neave, G., *Patterns of Equality*, NFER, 1976.

Nickell, S., 'Education and Lifetime Patterns of Unemployment', *Journal of Political Economy*, Vol. 87, No. 5, Pt 2, 1979, pp. S117–S131.

O'Donoghue, M., *Economic Dimensions in Education*, Gill & MacMillan, 1971.

OECD, *Trends in Educational Expenditure in the OECD Countries*, Paris, 1978.

Office of Population Census & Statistics, *Birth Statistics England & Wales*, HMSO, 1981.

Office of Population Census & Statistics, *Population Trends*, HMSO, 1982.

Ollerenshaw, K., *Returning to Teaching*, Report of a Research Project, Dept of Educational Research, Lancaster University, 1973, p. 5.

Open University, *The Finance of Education*, Course ED322 Educational Studies and Social Science, 1977.

Open University, *Providing the Teachers*, unit 8 of course E222, The Control of Education in Britain, 1979.

Parnes, H. S., 'Manpower Analysis in Educational Planning', in Blaug, M., ed., *Economics of Education 1*, Penguin, 1968.

Parsons, D. O., 'The Cost of School Time: Foregone Earnings and Human Capital Formation', *Journal of Political Economy*, Vol. 82, No. 2, Pt 1, March/April 1974, pp. 251–66.

Peacock, A. T., and Wiseman, J., *Education for Democrats*, Institute of Economic Affairs, 1964.

Peacock, A. and Wiseman, J., 'Principles of Educational Finance in Developed Countries', in Blaug, M., ed., *Economics of Education 2*, Penguin, 1969.

Peston, M., 'Accountability in Education: Some Economic Aspects', *Education Policy Bulletin*, Vol. 8, No. 2, Autumn 1980, pp. 115–26.

Prest, A. R. and Turvey, R., 'Cost-Benefit Analysis: a Survey', *Economic Journal*, Vol. 75, December 1965, pp. 683–735.

Psacharopoulos, G., *Returns to Education: An International Comparison*, Elsevier, 1973.

Psacharopoulos, G., *Earnings and Education in OECD Countries*, OECD, Paris, 1975.

Psacharopoulos, G., 'The Perverse Effects of Public Subsidisation of Education', *Comparative Education Review*, Vol. 21, No. 1, February 1977, pp. 69–89.

Psacharopoulos, G., 'Family Background, Education and Achievement', *British Journal of Sociology*, September 1977.

Psacharopoulos, G. and Layard, R., 'Human Capital and Earnings: British Evidence and a Critique', *Review of Economic Studies*, Vol. XLVI, No. 3, July 1979, pp. 485–504.

Pyle, D., 'Resource Allocation in Education', *Social and Economic Administration*, Vol. 10, No. 2, Summer 1976, pp. 106–22.

Ranson, S., 'Changing Relations between Centre and Locality in Education', *Local Government Studies*, Vol. 6, No. 6, November/December 1980, pp. 3–23.

Razin, A., 'Economic Growth and Education: New Evidence', *Economic Development and Cultural Change*, Vol. 25, January 1977, pp. 317–324.

Rhodes, R. A. W., *Control and Power in Central–Local Government Relations*, SSRC, Gower, 1981.

Robbins Report, *Report of the Committee on Higher Education*, Cmnd 2154, HMSO, 1963.

Robinson, E. A. G. and Vaizey, J., eds, *Economics of Education*, MacMillan, 1966.

Ross, D. H. and McKenna, B., *Class Size: the Multi Dollar Question*, Teachers College, Columbia University, NY, 1955.

Ross, J. M., *et al.*, *A Critical Appraisal of Comprehensive Education*, NFER, 1972.

Rubenstein, D., ed., *Education and Equality*, Penguin, 1979.

Rumberger, R. W., *Overeducation in the US Labour Market*, Praeger, 1981.

Sabulao, C. M. and Hickrod, G. A., 'Optimum Size of School Districts relative to selected costs', *Journal of Educational Administration*, Vol. IX, No. 2, October 1971, pp. 178–92.

Schultz, T. W., 'Education and Economic Growth' in Henry, N. B., ed., *Social Forces Influencing American Education*, University of Chicago Press, 1961.

Scott, M., 'Investment in Education in the UK 1951–1971', *Oxford Review of Education*, Vol. 6, No. 1, 1980, pp. 21–30.

Secondary Heads Association, *Big and Beautiful*, London, 1979.

Simkins, T., *Economics and the Management of Resources*, Sheffield, Papers in Education Management, Sheffield Polytechnic, 1981.

Smith, C. Selby, *The Costs of Further Education*, Pergamon, 1970.

Smith, R., 'Comprehensive Schools: the Problem of Appropriate Size', in *A Volume of Essays for Elizabeth Halsall*, eds, Brock, C. and Ryba, R., University of Hull Institute of Education, 1980.

Smith, R. E., 'The Opportunity Cost of Participating in a Training Programme', *Journal of Human Resources*, Vol. vi, No. 4, Fall 1971, pp. 510–19.

Stone, R., 'Whittling away at the Residual – some thoughts on Denison's Growth Accounting', *Journal of Economic Literature*, Vol. XVIII, December 1980, pp. 1539–43.

Taylor, G. and Ayres, N., *Born and Bred Unequal*, Longman, 1970.

Taylor, W., *Heading for Change*, HTV Publications, Cardiff, 1969.

Thomas, H. R., 'Cost-effectiveness Analysis as a Method of Assessing 'A' Level Performance in Different Educational Establishments', *Educational Studies*, Vol. 7, No. 2, 1981, pp. 95–103.

Thurow, L., 'Education and Economic Equality', *Public Interest*, 1972, reprinted in Baxter, C., *et al.*, eds, *Economics and Education Policy*, Longman, 1977.

Tunley, P., Travers, T. and Pratt, J., *Depriving the Deprived*, Kogan Page, 1979.

UNESCO, *Statistical Yearbook*, 1981.

Vaizey, J., *Economics of Education*, Faber & Faber, 1962.

Vaizey, J., *The Political Economy of Education*, Duckworth, 1972.

Vaizey, J., 'The School in Question: an Economists viewpoint', *Oxford Review of Education*, Vol. 5, No. 3, October 1979, pp. 207–14.

Vaizey, J. and Sheehan, J., *Resources for Education*, Allen & Unwin, 1968.

Vaizey, J., Hewton, E. and Norris, K., *The Costs of New Education Technologies*, Gulbenkian Institute, Lisbon, 1971.

Vinokur, A., 'Economic Analysis of Lifelong Education' in Dave, R. H., ed., *Foundations of Lifelong Education*, Pergamon Press, 1976.

Wagner, L., 'Vouchers – are they the answer for parental choice?; *Education*, Vol. 144, No. 24, 13th December 1974.

Wagner, L., 'The Measurement of Output' in *The Internal Efficiency of Educational Institutions*, Open University Course ED 322, 1977.

Wagner, L., *The Economics of Educational Media*, Macmillan, 1982.

Webb, P. C., 'Teaching Cost Models for Sixth Forms', *Educational Policy Bulletin*, Vol. 7, No. 1, Spring 1979, pp. 43–65.

Weiler, D., *et al.*, *A Public School Voucher Demonstration: The First Year at Alum Rock*, Rand, California, 1974.

Weisbrod, B. A., *External Benefits of Public Education*, Princeton, 1964.

West, E. G., *Economics, Education and the Politician*, Institute of Economic Affairs, 1968.

West, E. G., 'Tom Paine's Voucher Scheme for Public Education', *Southern Economic Journal*, Vol. 33, January 1967, pp. 378–82.

West, E. G., *Education and the State*, Institute of Economic Affairs, 2nd Ed., 1970.

Whitehead, A. K., 'Screening and Education: A Theoretical and Empirical Study', *British Review of Economic Issues*, Vol. 3, No. 8, Spring 1981, pp. 844–62.

Williams, G., 'Educational Planning, Past, Present and Future', *Educational Policy Bulletin*, Vol. 7, No. 2, Autumn 1979, pp. 125–40.

Williams, G., Blackstone, T. and Metcalf, D., *The Academic Labour Market*, Elsevier, 1974.

Williams, G. and Gordon, A., 'Perceived Earnings Functions and ex ante Rates of Return to Post Compulsory Education in England', *Higher Education*, Vol. 10, 1981, pp. 199–227.

Wilson, B., ed., *Education Equality and Society*, Allen & Unwin, 1975.

Wilson, R. A., 'The Rate of Return to becoming a Qualified Scientist or Engineer in Great Britain 1966–1976', *Scottish Journal of Political Economy*, Vol. 27, No. 1, February 1980, pp. 41–62.

Wise, O. A., 'Academic Achievement and Job Performance', *American Economic Review*, Vol. 65, No. 3, June 1973, pp. 350–365.

Wiseman, J., 'The Economics of Education', *Scottish Journal of Political Economy*, Vol. 6, No. 1, 1959, pp. 48–58.

Woodhall, M., 'The Economic Returns to Investment in Women's Education', *Higher Education*, Vol. 2, 1973, pp. 275–300.

Woodhall, M., 'The Arguments for and against Loans', in Baxter, C., *et al.*, *Economics and Education Policy: a reader*, Longman, 1977.

Woodhall, M., 'Alternatives in the Finance of Education: Vouchers' in *The Finance of Education*, Block IV of Economics and Education Policy, Open University, 1977.

Woodhall, M., '*Student Loans: Lessons from Recent International Experience*', Policy Studies Institute, London, 1982.

Wright, M., 'From Planning to Control: PESC in the 1970s in Wright, M., ed., *Public Spending Decisions: Growth and Restraint in the 1970s*, Allen & Unwin, 1980.

Wright, M., ed., *Public Spending Decisions: Growth and Restraint in the 1970s*, Allen & Unwin, 1980.

Wykstra, R. A., *Human Capital Formation and Manpower Development*, Free Press, 1971.

Zabalza, A., Turnbull, P. and Williams, G., *The Economics of Teacher Supply*, Cambridge University Press, 1979.

Ziderman, A., 'Does it Pay to Take a Degree', *Oxford Economic Papers*, Vol. 25, No. 2, July 1973, pp. 262–74.

Index